The Old Mermaids Book
of Days and Nights

Also by Kim Antieau

Old Mermaids Books
The Blue Tail • *Church of the Old Mermaids* • *The First Book of Old Mermaids Tales* • *The Fish Wife* • *An Old Mermaid Journal* • *The Old Mermaids Book of Days and Nights: A Year and a Day Journal* • *The Old Mermaids Oracle* • *The Second Book of Old Mermaids Tales*

Other Novels
Broken Moon • *Butch* • *Coyote Cowgirl* • *Deathmark* • *The Desert Siren* • *Her Frozen Wild* • *The Gaia Websters* • *Jewelweed Station* • *The Jigsaw Woman* • *Maternal Instincts* • *Mercy, Unbound* • *The Monster's Daughter* • *Queendom: Feast of the Saints* • *The Rift* • *Ruby's Imagine* • *Swans in Winter* • *Whackadoodle Times* • *Whackadoodle Times Two*

Other Nonfiction
Answering the Creative Call • *Certified: Learning to Repair Myself and the World in the Emerald City* • *Counting on Wildflowers: An Entanglement* • *MommaEarth Goddess Runes* • *The Salmon Mysteries: a Reimagining of the Eleusinian Mysteries* • *The Salmon Mysteries Workbook: Reimagining the Eleusinian Mysteries* • *Under the Tucson Moon*

Other Collections
Entangled Realities (with Mario Milosevic) • *Haunted* • *Tales Fabulous and Fairy* • *Trudging to Eden*

Chapbook
Blossoms

Blog
www.kimantieau.com

Photography
www.kimantieau.smugmug.com

The Old Mermaids Book of Days and Nights

*A Daily Guide to the Magic and Inspiration
of the Old Sea, the New Desert, and Beyond*

Kim Antieau

The Old Mermaids Book of Days and Nights
by Kim Antieau

Copyright © 2012 by Kim Antieau

ISBN: 978-1-949644-46-3

All rights reserved.

No part of this book may be reproduced
without written permission of the author.

Cover image, "She Was Half Wild," by Nancy Norman.
Cover and book design by Mario Milosevic.

http://www.kimantieau.com

Electronic editions of this book are
available at most ebook store.

Published by Green Snake Publishing
www.greensnakepublishing.com

in memory of my mother,
Mary Kelly Antieau,
who was an Old Mermaid at heart,
and for
Delia, Ellen, and Terri,
who made it all possible

Origins

I can't be sure, but I believe this book might be the one the Old Mermaids put together when they lived in the Old Mermaids Sanctuary after the Old Sea dried up and they made their home in the New Desert. Sometimes they needed reminders of how to live, how to be, how to laugh and dance. So they went out into the desert at dawn, at dusk, in the middle of the night, and they gathered together the wisdom you'll find in this book.

They pulled this word out of the dry desert air and that word from the flooded wash during the monsoons. They coaxed this sentence from a chorus of coyotes howling love songs at the moon, and they found that sentence shimmering in the dew on a spider web near where the Old Woman and Old Man of the Mountains lived. They enticed this story from the bark of the Old Sycamore, and the Old Saguaros whispered that story to them the night their flowers bloomed and the bats came out to drench themselves in nectar.

Every word, every sentence, every story here is meant for you, for each of you, to heal, to amuse, and to mystify, to remind you that you are loved and you are swimming in your own divinely perfect self. You are magic and so are the Old Mermaids.

The Old Mermaids remind us to swim, dance, walk, play, love, and create in beauty. It is the Old Mermaid Way.

—Kim Antieau
novice, Church of the Old Mermaids

January 1

"She who laughs a lot laughs a lot."
—*Sister Laughs A Lot Mermaid*

January 2

Sometimes I feel the Wild pulsing in my own soul and I know it is Nature speaking to me, through me. I feel as though my creative force and my passion for the world is Nature working her art through me: I am her art piece.

—*Under the Tucson Moon*

January 3

"Sister Ruby Rosarita Mermaid adjusted to life in the New Desert after the Old Sea dried up more quickly than the other Old Mermaids. Of course she missed the Old Sea and all that was within. But she knew the Old Sea was in the clouds, her blood, and in every cell of the Old Salmon who made their way up and down various creeks and rivers. So it wasn't that she didn't love the Old Sea as much as the other Old Mermaids; it was that she loved the New Desert, too.

—*The First Book of Old Mermaids Tales*

January 4

"Someone once told me that when we lose our dreams, the land dreams for us."

—*The Desert Siren*

January 5

"Actually, it wasn't quite a house yet. The Old Mermaids were still building it, with the help of some neighbors. They used mud and straw and stone—all materials from the old dried up sea. As they built the house, they let the mud and straw and stone tell them stories. They listened to what the cacti and coyotes and crows had to say, too. The neighbors had more stories. The stories made the work easier, and the house seemed to like the stories. It shaped itself beautifully around them and this land. It was a piece of art."

—Church of the Old Mermaids

January 6

Sara's breathing quickened. She felt strangely happy. She remembered other times when her mother had gone down to the beach without Sara and her sisters, times before a storm. Even then, Sara had felt as though she should be with her—her place was with her mother singing to the sea.

—The Fish Wife

January 7

"Perhaps a journey up the mountains will do," Sister Bea Wilder Mermaid said.
        —*The Second Book of Old Mermaids Tales*

January 8

"She kissed me," Murphy said. "Then she bent over and picked up the most beautiful shell I've ever seen—tiny and shaped in a spiral—and she said, 'You know what this means, don't you?' I shook my head. She pressed the seashell into my hand. 'Whenever you find a seashell it means a mermaid has found her tail and is free again.' And then she dove back to the sea and swam away. I never saw her again."

—The Fish Wife

January 9

"Today I was remembering my old Scottish grandmother. Whenever she saw us or whenever we left her presence, she gave us a blessing. 'May the strength of the oak trees be thine,' she would say. Or 'excellence of travel be on you.' So today I would like to say to you: Joy of night and day be yours. Joy of sun and moon be yours. Joy of all the wildflowers be yours. And may the love and affection of the entire world be yours as all of my love and affection is already yours."

—*Jewelweed Station*

January 10

Grand Mother Yemaya Mermaid was excited by the prospect of creating thirteen comforters for the Old Mermaids. It is said—although I can't be sure it's true—that she began by asking the Invisibles of the place if she could please find and pick up pieces of the desert to use to create the quilts. And so she gathered up leaves from the mountains and forests. She found branches there, too, and the bones of many creatures. She gathered up feathers and the whispers of dreams on her way down. On the floor of the desert, she found prickly pear pads and the skeletons of cacti. She gathered up the clucking of the quail and the hooting of the owl. She found flat rocks, more feathers, and the songs of coyotes. One day she found seashells in the wash. She kept looking until she had thirteen. Finally she sat under the night sky and caught the dust of falling stars. She scooped up moonlight at the same time.
—*The First Book of Old Mermaids Tales*

January 11

Moon Day. A butterfly the color of my name did tell me that a Big Spin was coming our way. I was standing by Mr. Grant's wisteria, which hung over his fence and down into our yard, when Ruby Butterfly, this jeweled metamorphosis of a cattypillar, landed on a bright green wisteria leaf like some kind of winged oracle and looked straight at me; we exchanged glances, you know the way liked-minded and soul-bodied creatures can. We understood each other down deep to our transfigured and transforming cellular parts.

—*Ruby's Imagine*

January 12

"The whisper is meant only for you. You must follow it to its source."

—*The First Book of Old Mermaids Tales*

January 13

"Things don't always turn out all right, but they always turn out."

—*Church of the Old Mermaids*

January 14

We would gather into circles, or spirals, depending upon the mood of the community, and give thanks, dance, bless ourselves, and draw the moon down into our hearts. I would stare up into the face of the moon and drink her down until I was full of her light.

—*The Jigsaw Woman*

January 15

A day or a week or a month or a lifetime later, Grand Mother Yemaya Mermaid completed the quilts. As she gazed at them covering the desert floor, she wondered—for just a second—how these rough prickly pieces of the desert were ever going to bring comfort to anyone. She thanked Grandmother Spider and all the creatures of the New Desert. She picked up the quilts one by one and carefully folded them. By the time she was finished, it was night and all the Old Mermaids were sleeping. She took the quilts into the house and to each Old Mermaid. Every quilt was made from different pieces of the desert, of course, and Grand Mother Yemaya Mermaid had sewn a little extra into each one.
—*The First Book of Old Mermaids Tales*

January 16

"I remember Sister Faye Mermaid telling Tulip once that it was just polite to thank the wind, the sun, the water, the earth, the birds, the cacti—to thank all the elements of life, thank them for their gifts, to express our love for them. So that is what I am doing: thanking the elemental Old Mermaids for all your gifts."

—*The First Book of Old Mermaids Tales*

January 17

"When a person knows who she really is, once she understands her true wild oceanic self, she discovers her Old Mermaid self."

—*Church of the Old Mermaids*

January 18

This morning we awakened to rain. We went out into a glorious cool morning, and I could smell the rain. Or I could smell the desert after a rain. What a miracle it was to be able to smell. And there is nothing like the desert after a rain. Everything is plump and juicy and ecstatic. I told Mario it's like being in a world where everyone and everything got lucky the night before.

—Under the Tucson Moon

January 19

"It's no dream, luv," Murphy said. He opened his arms, and Sara ran into them. They held each other for a long while. When they let each other go, flowers were blooming from the green and water was tickling their toes.

—The Fish Wife

January 20

Grandma Crow said the Wind always told the truth, no matter what direction it came from. "That's where you go for answers," she told Butch. And if you couldn't understand the Wind, ask Eagle to translate. Or Cottonwood. Or Rattlesnake. Only stand far back from Rattlesnake. He was related to Grandma No One and could strike out at you, even as he was telling the truth.

—*Butch: A Bent Western*

January 21

The Lady shook her head. *"Cher,* we just got to take care of ourselves somehow. Even when this is all done. I heard once someone say that if we lose our awe of things, then everything is for sale. Maybe we lost our awe for Nature, our awe for our lives, so everything is for sale: our air, our water, our planet, each other. You, Ruby, you've always had that awe. You can see how things can be different, better. You can see the truth. Hang on to that, dawlin'."

—*Ruby's Imagine*

January 22

The women got closer to the water or the water got closer to them. In the semi-darkness, a wave of light filtered through the storm, and the beach shuddered and shimmered. Suddenly Sara saw the women for what they truly were, saw their tails gleam and glimmer, and she looked down and saw her own true self.

— *The Fish Wife*

January 23

She loved plants. Was there anything on creation that was more amazing than plants? They ate sunlight. They converted sunlight into food. They were, essentially, sunlight, in all its various guises, brought down to earth.

—*Jewelweed Station*

January 24

"The Old Mermaids themselves are betwixt and between."

— *Church of the Old Mermaids*

January 25

Mom took me to a shop at the Flea we hadn't seen before: Siren Song. It was filled with wooden mermaids that looked like they had been on the masthead of some old ship or on the altar of some old church. The woman who ran the shop stood with her hands on her hips looking at me almost the entire time we were there. I liked the attention.

"Do I know you?" she asked me.

I shook my head. "No one knows me."

"Ah, a philosopher," the woman said. "You're fourteen going on four hundred." She nodded. "I know your kind. Here's my advice to you, sugar. Go with the flow—but watch out for waterfalls."

—*The Blue Tail*

January 26

"I remember when we first left the Old Sea," Sister Sophia Mermaid said. "We were all so sad. We felt like there was nothing we could do. We were lost, and we felt homeless. We missed the Old Sea. One day I happened to see a bobcat in the wash. She just stepped down into the sand and stared at me. Then she started walking away. She stopped and looked back at me as if to say, 'This way to the promised land.' Isn't that what we're all looking for?"

"Either that or the promised sea," Sister Ruby Rosarita Mermaid said.

—*The First Book of Old Mermaids Tales*

January 27

I said, "You're going down to the beach this late? Won't it be dark soon?"

Annie nodded. "Sure," she said. "That's the best time to see the mermaids."

—*The Blue Tail*

January 28

"Yes, I see it," Herman said. "I see all kinds of animals and plants here with you. A jaguar, too. Sat right over there." He pointed to a spot by the water. "The madrone watches over lost souls, you must realize. As soon as your mother left her body, she went right to that tree. Became that tree. Can't you feel her? I bet you returned here again and again and you heard stories at her feet, didn't you? At her roots. A jackrabbit sat over there, far from the jaguar. And the cottonwood tree kept the sun off you."

—*Butch: A Bent Western*

January 29

Sister Laughs A Lot Mermaid was next. She said, "I gift you with a wicked and wonderful sense of humor and with the ability to laugh."
—*The Second Book of Old Mermaids Tales*

January 30

Water flowed through a pale blue fish that a pink mermaid with a green tail was holding. The mermaid was looking up and laughing.

"What is this?" Sara asked. "What are all of these?"

Renaud stopped and turned around. "They're mermaids," he said. "Didn't I mention that Mameau is one of *Les Sirènes?* The sirens. She is one of the beauties from the island. They say she and the others like her were created to seduce white men. I don't believe it. It's her gift. We all have gifts. Hers is beauty."

—*The Fish Wife*

January 31

Her life was about turning trash into beauty.
—*Church of the Old Mermaids*

February 1

The mermaid on my wall was not a young mermaid. Or a little one. Her shoulder length hair flipped up at the end, and her green eyes were wild-looking. Her entire expression was wild—as if any moment she was going to leap, swim, or dive off that canvas into my room and take me on some kind of adventure.

—The Blue Tail

February 2

"All that you see, Daughter Keelie," my mother said, "is a part of you. The hills, valleys, trees, stones, all manners of creatures, crawling, flying, walking, they are you. Treat all as you would wish to be treated."

—The Jigsaw Woman

February 3

"And one day the Artists came and did what they suppose to do in times like these: answer the call of the land, the community, and make beauty out of destruction, out of their imagines, out of what had been and was now. That's what they did."

—*Ruby's Imagine*

February 4

Grand Mother Yemaya Mermaid whispered to Sister Faye Mermaid, "Into your quilt I sewed knowledge of peace and desert magic."

—*The First Book of Old Mermaids Tales*

February 5

Mother Star Stupendous Mermaid took the New Woman into the desert. They didn't walk far. Just far enough.

"Now be still," Mother Star Stupendous Mermaid said.

"But then all I will hear is the roar," she said.

"Then listen to it," Mother Star Stupendous Mermaid said. . . .

Mother Star Stupendous Mermaid left the New Woman. We glanced out at her a few times. We could tell she wanted to bolt, to run, to keep going, going, going. Gone. But she was learning what we all must learn: We can't run from the roaring inside.

When it became night in the desert, the New Woman returned to us. "I am learning the language of my soul," she said. "The trees, birds, bees, wind, the coyotes and lynxes—they are all helping me with the translation."

Later, we all went into the desert night and held hands with the stars.

—*The Second Book of Old Mermaids Tales*

February 6

The Old Owl is here, quail flutter as we walk the property, and I find bobcat prints in the wash. Magic awaits. I know it. Or I used to know it. We'll see.

—*Under the Tucson Moon*

February 7

"Why don't you ask the Old Mermaids?"
—*Church of the Old Mermaids*

February 8

Then one night Betty remembers waking up and hearing her mother and father out under the moon, over by an agave plant, singing and rattling and praying. She fell back to sleep the way children do. She couldn't be sure, but she thinks it was the next morning when she awakened feeling warm and comforted. She lay in her bed savoring this wonderful sensation for several minutes before she realized she was covered in a quilt. She pulled it off and looked at it. It looked as though someone had sewn pieces of the desert together with an almost translucent blue thread: leaves, prickly pear pads, bones, feathers. Yet when she touched it, it was cloth—beautiful, soft, warm cloth.

—*The First Book of Old Mermaids Tales*

February 9

Grand Mother Yemaya Mermaid said, "We gift you with the ability to embrace and love your true self. This will require practice and commitment, but the way will be easier now because you will know you have been gifted and you've always been gifted."
—*The Second Book of Old Mermaids Tales*

February 10

"Now, go. I must sweep away any spirits left over from last night. I don't want to accidentally sweep you away."
—*Coyote Cowgirl*

February 11

"My parents told me that stars were really the teardrops of a giant who has lost her way."

—*An Old Mermaid Sanctuary*

February 12

"I gift you with friends," Sister Lyra Musica Mermaid said, "and the ability to discern who is good for you and who is not."

—*The Second Book of Old Mermaids Tales*

February 13

"Oh, sweetheart," I said, "you can see so many things at night that are hidden during the daylight. Look, night is the only time you can see the ashy skin of the sky."

—*Ruby's Imagine*

February 14

Grand Mother Yemaya Mermaid was the first there. The shiny blue cloth of her dress sparkled in the sunlight and looked for a moment like two tails trailing behind her—or as if she were actually swimming through the air rather than walking.

—*The Second Book of Old Mermaids Tales*

February 15

"Remember," Sister Ruby Rosarita Mermaid said. "You have companions all around: in the wind, in the woods, in the sky. Be nourished. Be full of yourself."
—*The Second Book of Old Mermaids Tales*

February 16

"We are all gifted when we are born," Mother Star Stupendous Mermaid said, "but we often forget, because of life, because of time. Just because. Now we will help you remember."

—*The Second Book of Old Mermaids Tales*

February 17

Sister Sophia Mermaid said, "She has the wisdom in her. It will come."
—*The Second Book of Old Mermaids Tales*

February 18

Rattleday

It is so quiet. I hear the wind lifting the dry palm leaves and shaking them. It sounds a bit like the rattle Sissy Maggie Mermaid made out of a dried gourd one year. Only bigger. It was a storm rattle. Sissy Maggie stood outside with that rattle and danced for a long while, until a Storm did come to see what all the noise was about. The desert breathed moist that night.

—*The First Book of Old Mermaids Tales*

February 19

"I gift you with healing and magic."
—*The Second Book of Old Mermaids Tales*

February 20

"Get the starfish outta your eyes, sister."
—*Sister Sheila Na Giggles Mermaid*

February 21

We walked timeless across the forests and deserts and jungles and plains. We walked the Earth. Blessed the Earth. Were blessed by her.

I held out my hand and all the people climbed onto me. Ate from me. Blessed me. Blessed themselves. Made love. Food. Babies. All was sacred. I lay down on the Earth and was the Earth. I was alive with all that was sacred. Which was all.

—*The Jigsaw Woman*

February 22

The paint had faded, but the mermaids were still discernible, swimming on the ruined walls, their tails and hair sometimes entwined with the tail and hair of another mermaid. Some of them had hair so white it was nearly indistinguishable from the walls. Others had red hair, blue, yellow, black, brown. Some were old. Some were new. They had different skin tones and shades. They were different sizes, different personalities. No one mermaid dominated, although one in the middle, with long graying red hair, looked straight out at them.

—*An Old Mermaid Sanctuary*

February 23

The Old Man reached his hand down into the dirt. He went deep, deep, deep. Finally he pulled his arm and hand out of the earth and said, "This will help you be in the here and now. The past is done; the future is an illusion. Hold out your hand."

The New Woman held out her hand. The Old Man dropped a black stone into her palm.

—*The Second Book of Old Mermaids Tales*

February 24

Lily handed Myla her ball of thread. "You keep it," Lily said. "I might lose it. Or a cactus faery might snatch it from me. Or a coyote might sing a song I really like so I'd give it to him in thanks. Or a hummingbird might want to use it in her nest. Or a spider might decide it wants a web made out of red hair. You never know."

—*An Old Mermaid Sanctuary*

February 25

"Is this where the Old Mermaids live?"
—*Church of the Old Mermaids*

February 26

Sister Lyra Musica Mermaid got a bowl of rice and scooped out black beans from a big pot and poured the beans over the rice. She handed the bowl to Sister Ruby Rosarita Mermaid who handed it to the New Woman.

"Eat," Sister Ruby Rosarita Mermaid said.

Grand Mother Yemaya Mermaid nodded. "You must always eat when you go to any other land, faery or otherwise."

"But won't that mean I can never go home?" the New Woman asked.

Sister Sheila Na Giggles Mermaid laughed. "You are home, darlin'," she said.

—*The Second Book of Old Mermaids Tales*

February 27

"You ask me to tell you about love?
Showing is so much better."
—*Sister Magdelene Mermaid*

February 28

She put her hand on the wooden door knob, turned it, and pushed it open just as someone on the other side pulled it open. A tall woman the color of the night sky smiled and opened her arms to her.
—*The Second Book of Old Mermaids Days*

February 29

"You know what Sister Laughs A Lot Mermaid did? She untied him right there and then. She said, 'Grand Mother Yemaya Mermaid was right. You're a wild thing. Now go be wild.' At first Rocky the Crow did not know what to do. Finally, the Old Mermaids lay on the desert floor looking up at the sky. Crow eventually followed their gaze and saw the sky again. He stared for a long while, and then he shuddered, as if he had suddenly been filled up with wonder or love for the sky. He flapped his wings and flew away."

—*Church of the Old Mermaids*

March 1

"You and your mother are sea fairies, sea goddesses, and as such, you must find your own way home again."
—*The Fish Wife*

March 2

"The rest is . . . mystery."
—*Sister Faye Mermaid*

March 3

"Everyone has a siren song. . . . It's whatever you do that you love completely. Something fluid, beautiful, all yours."

—*Church of the Old Mermaids*

March 4

"In the Old Sea, every young Old Mermaid has a Gifted ceremony, and her mermothers bestow on her various gifts. That's being Gifted."
—*The Second Book of Old Mermaids Tales*

March 5

"Any town that has mermaids is considered a lucky town. Our mermaids hung out at Siren Rock. When it was gone, they went away. Or so everyone believes. Everyone but me. I swear, on some Full Moon and New Moon nights I can see them. Or I think I will see them."

—*The Blue Tail*

March 6

Sister Ruby Rosarita Mermaid kept stirring. She did not tell them this was the first time she had ever made storytelling soup because she knew something could be real and meaningful before it ever existed. "Carrots, carrots, with all your fine merits, help make this stew a healing brew."

—*The First Book of Old Mermaids Tales*

March 7

Her mother had told her people usually didn't notice jewelweed. That was because it usually grew with other jewelweed. One flower or one plant did not stand out. Instead they were all tangled up with one another. It was a wonderful kind of masquerade. To be disguised amongst all those who looked just like you.

—*Jewelweed Station*

March 8

"I've heard it said that you can ask the wild bees what the druid knows," Sister Lyra Musica Mermaid whispered as the bees hummed all around them.

"Then we'll just hear back what we told the druids," Sister Bea Wilder Mermaid said.

The Old Mermaids chuckled in time to the beebop.

—*The First Book of Old Mermaids Tales*

March 9

"Old people, especially old women, were beautiful like the moon . . . those with moon beauty knew more secrets because they knew about things and places where the sun did not shine."

—*Church of the Old Mermaids*

March 10

Myla closed her eyes and breathed in Lily's song. When Lily stopped humming, Myla opened her eyes; she looked to her left and then to her right. There. Someone was crossing the wash. Several someones. Shimmering in the moonlight. Did each of them wear a ghost of a tail? One of them waved. Myla recognized her, didn't she? From her dream so long ago. Myla waved. She blinked. The wash was empty again. The night was rich with moon beauty.

—*Church of the Old Mermaids*

March 11

And then she heard the whispering again. This time she recognized it. It was the whispering of her own being. It was the whisper of the Old Sea pulsing inside her—pulsing inside every living being.

—*The First Book of Old Mermaids Tales*

March 12

"All good conversation is the search for truth."
—*Church of the Old Mermaids*

March 13

"She Who Was Before exists in your body," Sula said. "Move with her, sing with her. Be her. Become yourself—be *full* of your*self*."

—*Her Frozen Wild*

March 14

"With our breath, we combine earth, sun, and tears," Sister Faye Mermaid chanted. "Transforming our fears and tears into house and home."

—*The First Book of Old Mermaids Tales*

March 15

That night, I dreamed I saw a group of women chanting and dancing in a circle. I decided I couldn't join them, but one woman called me forward. As soon as they linked hands with me, the circle disintegrated. Then the world was coming to a cataclysmic end: thunder, lightning, earthquakes. I was in a huge room with hundreds of people. I said we should all hold hands and dance. That would save the world. Of course I couldn't get them all to dance, and I was certain now all would end, but I kept dancing anyway and soon the apocalypse stopped. It had worked even though I hadn't done it right. The world was saved.
—*Tales Fabulous and Fairy*

March 16

"Seaweed, seaweed, fill our needs. From the sea, from the sea, let it be, let it be, blessed sea."
—*The First Book of Old Mermaids Tales*

March 17

The girls grew and flourished in the sanctuary. They collected rocks and seashells. They found seashells in the wash every spring after the river dried up. No one understood where the shells had come from, but everyone agreed they must be a gift from the auld ma and the auld sea for her dearest children.

—The Fish Wife

March 18

The Old Mermaids built the Tea Shell on the edge of the Old Mermaid Sanctuary where they had made their homes since the Old Sea dried up and they washed up on the shores of the New Desert like moon-beautiful pieces of driftwood. It was a small place, the Old Mermaids Tea Shell, much like the Old Mermaids art and writing studio. It was big enough to hold an Old Mermaid or two, three or four small round tables with a couple of chairs each, and shelf after shelf of teapots, teacups, and bottles of tea. Sister Sophia Mermaid wanted a place where fellow travelers of the New Desert could sit for a spell, relax, and sip a bit of tea.

—*The First Book of Old Mermaids Tales*

March 19

The New Woman looked at the pool again. The stars shimmered or a breeze rippled the water and she could see the mermaid painted on the bottom of the pool. The mermaid was motioning to her.
>   —*The Second Book of Old Mermaids Tales*

March 20

"Who you are is the who you were before someone told you you were a good girl because you stood still or were quiet and didn't speak your heart. Who you are is the who you were before someone told you to act like a lady which meant not to squirm, not to move, not to cry when you needed to mourn or sing when you were joyful. Who you are is the who you were before someone told you you weren't tall enough, short enough, skinny or pretty enough. Before anyone told you you were not right."

—*Her Frozen Wild*

March 21

"Aunt Delilah used to talk about our Irish relatives. She said it was a common belief amongst the Irish in their villages—especially the villages near the sea—that some of their people were descended from mermaids. Aunt Delilah called them sirens."

—*The Desert Siren*

March 22

"Your grandma Consuelo is a siren. She sings to the wild things, she wrangles sea horses and dust storms. She directs coyote choruses and bargains with ravens. She does not hear the call of the wild. She is the call of the wild."

—*The Desert Siren*

March 23

She stopped and gazed at the house growing up out of the ground as though it was a part of the land, only it had windows and a door. A blue door. The New Woman was certain if she opened that blue door, everything would change.

—*The Second Book of Old Mermaids Tales*

March 24

The Señorita stepped off the porch and into the desert. It was a warm night and the moon was up. The owl started asking, "Who, who, who." The Señorita knew—now—that it would fly away soon, to go hunting, and return in the morning. If she could learn the habits of an owl in only three days, what else could she learn?

—Tales Fabulous and Fairy

March 25

The cactus had found a good companion in the mesquite. Very grounded. Rooted. Mesquite had the deepest root system of any tree, Myla knew. Someone had once found a live mesquite root 160 feet beneath the surface, in a copper mine. She put her hand on its trunk. Mesquite trees knew how to hold their ground. Old souls, she thought when she saw one like this, crouched toward the desert floor yet still reaching out to the world around it.

—*Church of the Old Mermaids*

March 26

"Ahhh, well, no one can know for sure, but they say this bottle was filled with water from the Old Sea where the Old Mermaids made their home before it dried up. And before it all went away, Sister Bridget Mermaid had the presence of mind to fill a couple of empty bottles they found along the shore with sea water. This one they put in the kitchen. Sometimes when the Old Mermaids were aching for the Old Sea, they came into the kitchen to gaze at the bottle, sometimes hold it. When the longing became too much, they took the stopper off and smelled the sea and remembered their lost friends and the life they had had to leave behind. They would even dab a drop behind their ears and onto their wrists, as though it were perfume, and of course, it was, to them. Sometimes their grief overwhelmed them and they wept as they held the open bottle. . . . Gradually the Old Mermaids realized they carried the Old Sea within them, always, just as you and I do."

 —*Church of the Old Mermaids*

March 27

"I gift you with stories."
—*The Second Book of Old Mermaids Tales*

March 28

"Does that belong to me?" Sister Ursula Divine Mermaid asked. She got up and walked to the tiny flame. The Old Bear took the flame onto her paw as she stood. It danced on her palm. She held it up to Sister Ursula Divine Mermaid's chest and then pressed it into her heart. It tickled, and Sister Ursula Divine Mermaid smiled. She felt warm. The warmth spread throughout her whole body. She shook herself until it all felt right.

—*The First Book of Old Mermaids Tales*

March 29

Last night Sister Lyra Musica Mermaid walked out into the desert and found the Moon fishing.
>　—*The First Book of Old Mermaids Tales*

March 30

"It's all right," Myla said. "I love having novices. . . . I am a novice as well. We generally don't barter at the Church of the Old Mermaids. Each gift of the wash—and therefore a gift from the Old Mermaids—is exactly what a particular person needs."

—*Church of the Old Mermaids*

March 31

"I've been telling you for years that I'm not doing anything," Myla said. "It's the beauty of the Old Mermaids flowing through me."

—*Church of the Old Mermaids*

April 1

"You are seeing everything from tired eyes," Sister Sophia Mermaid said. "You need to see things through old eyes, through Old Mermaid eyes for a while. Then you'll figure out a way to articulate what you've seen and what you know."

—*The First Book of Old Mermaids Tales*

April 2

After a time, the dragons gave way to wolves who ran beside them sometimes as men, sometimes as women. Sara ached to run with them. When Gabriel raised his gun to kill one of them, Renaud shouted, "Don't kill beauty, Gabriel. It will come back to haunt you."

—*The Fish Wife*

April 3

When I am in the Southwest, I feel loved and accepted. I walk amongst prickly plants here. They all have prickles. I rubbed mesquite leaves across my cheek yesterday. They were nearly as soft as mullein leaves. And right there by the leaves was a thorn. Could have cut my cheek deep if I'd rubbed my face a little differently.

Everything is prickly here with a soft center.

I can relate.

Just call me Briar Rose. Not because I fell to sleep for a hundred years, but because I am covered in thorns.

—*Under the Tucson Moon*

April 4

Sister Lyra Musica Mermaid showed the New Woman to her room. Sister Lyra Musica Mermaid said, "It's been waiting just for you."
—*The Second Book of Old Mermaids Tales*

April 5

When people asked Sister Ruby Rosarita Mermaid why her food was so special, she'd say, "I discovered the best spice of all: happenstance." Then she'd laugh.
—*The First Book of Old Mermaids Tales*

April 6

Grand Mother Yemaya Mermaid said, "Sometimes it feels as though we are far far from home. But today is not one of those days."

—*The First Book of Old Mermaids Tales*

April 7

"I know where the Old Mermaids are."
—*Church of the Old Mermaids*

April 8

"There are no rules, Ursula. No ten commandments on how to behave. This is not a thought experiment. Learn to be in your body; then you will discover who you truly are and the answers will come to you."

—*Her Frozen Wild*

April 9

Mother Star Stupendous Mermaid tried to reassure Sister Lyra Musica Mermaid. She encouraged her to go back into the wash. "Listen to the wind. Listen to the rocks. Listen to the birds. You will find your soul. It isn't lost. But you are. You'll find your way back to one another."
—*Church of the Old Mermaids*

April 10

"I gift you with the ability to be full of yourself," Sister Bea Wilder Mermaid said. "With the ability to be full of your true wild self." She kissed the top of the New Woman's head and the New Woman glimpsed a mountain lion in her mind's eye.

—*The Second Book of Old Mermaids Tales*

April 11

"It's no secret," Vesta said. "Any idiot can cook, can follow a recipe. But for the ingredients to transform into a wonderful meal, you have to have respect. The magic words come from you. From your own heart."

—*Coyote Cowgirl*

April 12

"Mermaids, mermaids, mermaids," Lily said.
—*Church of the Old Mermaids*

April 13

"Into your quilt," Grand Mother Yemaya Mermaid told Sister Laughs A Lot Mermaid, "I sewed the hugs of a forest full of giants."

—*The First Book of Old Mermaids Tales*

April 14

"Where did these wooden mermaids come from?" I asked.

"Portuguese artists carved them," she said. "They told me they were fishing someplace and these Old Mermaids were accidentally captured in fish nets. They're called 'old,' you know, because mermaids have been around forever. Anyway, these Old Mermaids agreed to sit for the artist while the ship turned around to take the mermaids back to their home sea. So in other words, no mermaids were harmed in the making of this art."

—*The Blue Tail*

April 15

"...if the light is just right or if you are a bit sleepy, you might be able to see the glitter of their tails. . . . And if you wake up and the darkness frightens you, remember Grand Mother Yemaya Mermaid is there with you. She is the darkness that protects you. Those flashes of color and light are just her mermaid tails."

—*Church of the Old Mermaids*

April 16

Take a deep breath. This is the wild. This is where you are most at home.

—*Under the Tucson Moon*

April 17

Sister Ursula Divine Mermaid walked deep into the desert to look for wild things. Road Runner ran by her.

"Can you tell if I am coming or going?" Road Runner asked.

"Does it matter?" she answered.
—*The First Book of Old Mermaids Tales*

April 18

"Did you ever notice when you cry, the grief begins to subside once you taste your own tears? That's because that sea water reminds the deepest truest part of you that you are always home, you are always with yourself, and that truth is comforting, even in the darkest times, even when you feel as though you are far from home, the way the Old Mermaids felt."

—*Church of the Old Mermaids*

April 19

"Some think that *abracadabra* means 'I create as I speak.' So it means we can create our world as we speak. Maybe every time we say something we are helping create our world. Like this place. It looks dark and scary to some people—and it smells bad from all the bad water. But I see it as a place where I met you and where people come to be safe and get food. Like a church. Or what they call a sanctuary. So we could name this the Lady's Sanctuary. That name puts more truth on it than just saying it's a dark and scary place."

—Ruby's Imagine

April 20

"This is the in-between place."
—*Church of the Old Mermaids*

April 21

"Do you think I am related to the Old Mermaids?" Lily asked.

"We're all related to the Old Mermaids," Myla said. "We're related by love."

—*An Old Mermaid Sanctuary*

April 22

"Who should she be full of if not herself?"
—*Church of the Old Mermaids*

April 23

"These seeds are beginnings, *cher*," the Lady With the Galaxy in Her Eye said. "They be blessed. You remember that."

—*Ruby's Imagine*

April 24

It rained so hard that day that many people claimed all the rivers, creeks, and washes flowed over their banks and made the desert the Old Sea again. As Sara watched the storm, the rain covered the windows. Or maybe the water rose and covered the whole house. Salmon swam past the house. Mermaids, too. There was the auld ma, motioning to her.

"The Old Mermaid is calling me," Sara said.

And just then her water broke. Her daughters were attempting to swim out of their own ocean and into this world.

—*The Fish Wife*

April 25

"She talks to the food. She says you must always talk to the spirits of the food. Ask their permission."

—*Coyote Cowgirl*

April 26

After this first batch of teas was so successful, Sister Sophia Mermaid decided to try something new. She went out into the desert in search of joy, love, peace, goodwill, laughter, and acceptance. The others went with her. They didn't have far to go. They set the jars down next to themselves and danced joyfully, loved each other, felt at peace, extended goodwill to one another, laughed themselves silly, and accepted that they had done a good thing.

—*The First Book of Old Mermaids Tales*

April 27

"I followed the bobcat, staying at a bit of distance," Sister Sophia Mermaid said. "I kept waiting for things to change or be different, or for something to happen. But nothing did. We just walked the wash, both of us looking side to side now and again. It was the same old wash. But after a while, I started wondering what she saw. What was the wash like to her? I squatted down a bit, I tried to feel the ground through my shoes, I breathed the desert air deeply. I did this for a while. I wondered if the bobcat was imagining herself as me. Maybe, maybe not. But I began to see the wash differently. I saw a cool spot under the paloverde, a great place to lounge out of the sun. And right there in that clear area, I could bask in the sun when it was cool. A rabbit hole. I could wait near and snatch me up a rabbit. I saw the wash as a bobcat saw the wash. And it was a different world. And the same. After a while, the bobcat went on her way, and I returned to the Old Mermaid Sanctuary and helped build our house."

—*The First Book of Old Mermaids Tales*

April 28

"Sisters," Coyote said, "I have watched you all morning and all afternoon. Please teach me this great magic."

"Coyote," White Sister said, "this is not your magic."

—*Tales Fabulous and Fairy*

April 29

She had walked for so long that she had forgotten she had once swam in the deep dark Old Sea with the Old Mermaids in the long ago time.
—*The Second Book of Old Mermaids Tales*

April 30

"Go with the flow—and watch out for waterfalls."
—*Sister Sophia Mermaid*

May 1

"We get to decide whether we step into the Old Sea where everything is possible. And the possible is everything. We are travelers, all of us. . . . And today, we seek the truth of the Old Mermaid Sanctuary."

—*Church of the Old Mermaids*

May 2

After an hour, a day, a week, or a month the New Woman and Sister Ruby Rosarita Mermaid came to a sign stuck on a pole in the ground that read: "Welcome to the Old Mermaids Sanctuary." They stepped over the threshold and walked toward the adobe house that slouched into the Sonora Desert as though it was a part of it, which, of course, it was. It slouched into the ground as though it was rooted there, which, of course, it was.

They walked through the door and into a room whose walls were covered in beautiful outdoor murals: mountains, rivers, oceans. . . . The Old Mermaids looked up and over at the New Woman and Sister Ruby Rosarita Mermaid when they came into the kitchen.

"At last!" they cried together. One by one they went to the New Woman and greeted her, hugged her, kissed her cheeks, and welcomed her.

—*The Second Book of Old Mermaids Tales*

May 3

Sister Ruby Rosarita Mermaid put her arm gently across the New Woman's shoulders and together they walked across the desert. They walked through a grove of old and new saguaro who seemed to bow slightly as they passed, a gesture that felt welcoming to the New Woman. They passed by jumping cholla that looked like tiny Kachina figures dancing in happiness because the New Woman had finally arrived at the Old Mermaids Sanctuary.
—*The Second Book of Old Mermaids Tales*

May 4

Sara sewed the girls' little dresses out of the same fabric. With every stitch she made, she sewed in protection and good health. When she was finished, she lit a candle and burned some of the herbs her mother had given to her. She made three pouches from the faery yarn. She dropped herbs and dirt and a shiny stone from the arroyo into them. Then she chanted to all the spirits who were listening.

—*The Fish Wife*

May 5

Sister Faye Mermaid handed the New Woman a mesquite pea pod. "Mesquite trees have the deepest roots of maybe any tree in the world. They are magical and beautiful. They grow in the desert and set their roots deep down into the Earth. . . . They find water wherever it is. They make a home wherever they grow. You can do that, too."

—*The Second Book of Old Mermaids Tales*

May 6

Then one night the Old Mermaids came to Myla in a dream. They swam the wash, which was filled with sea water, and motioned to her to join them. One of them reached down to the sandy bottom and pulled up an old glass bottle and held it out to her. When she awakened the next morning, she stumbled into the wash and found the same glass bottle—or one that looked like it. Her life changed in that instant. She felt as though she had heard the call of the wild—or the call of the Old Mermaids. The Church of the Old Mermaids was born that morning.

—*Church of the Old Mermaids*

May 7

"Ahhh, searching for the truth, then. Aren't you a little wet behind the ears for that?"
—*The First Book of Old Mermaids Tales*

May 8

Sara threw several threads into the arroyo. The Old Mermaids walked across the vast empty riverbed and found Sara's tossed threads after night fell again. The moon plucked out the silver threads. The sun wanted the green. The jaguar might have taken the orange and black. The wind sipped up some of the thread. The green cactus man made himself a new cap that bloomed like a flower.

—The Fish Wife

May 9

The New Woman gazed at the thirteen Old Mermaids. They looked young and old and in-between, with different colored hair and skin and eyes, their bodies big and little and in-between. They seemed familiar to her, like old friends, even though she did not think she had met them before this day.

—*The Second Book of Old Mermaids Tales*

May 10

I must leave this thorny palace, this refuge.
    So that I may be healed.
    May I be healed, may I be healed, may it be so.
    It is so.
    I wish the same for you.
                                 —*Under the Tucson Moon*

May 11

Tonight the wash was full of danger: gray and spooky. Last night it was full of magic: red and mystical. Probably the only thing different in the wash was me. One night I saw the talons of mortality swooping down on me and everyone I love. Another night the talons were nothing more than the artist's brush painting the night sky.

Maybe it's all a dream.

—Under the Tucson Moon

May 12

"I will tell you this, and then I will speak of it no more because I can see you don't believe me. But I will tell you, I was wrong—in the cave that day. I shouldn't have been afraid. I should have stayed. If someday you can find the wild in you, run with it, *duscha,* not away from it."

—*Her Frozen Wild*

May 13

"Into your quilt, I sewed the poetry of the stars and the moon," Grand Mother Yemaya Mermaid whispered to a sleeping Sister Bridget Mermaid.
 —*The First Book of Old Mermaids Tales*

May 14

"In our grief over the loss of the Old Sea, we sometimes forget that our bodies are containers of that sea. Our bodies are home."

—*Church of the Old Mermaids*

May 15

River maidens stared up at Sara from their watery homes. When Juan stood beside her and saw them, too, she knew he was a kindred spirit.

She said, "You can always tell a river maiden from a human woman. If some piece of a woman's clothing is almost always wet, then she is most likely born of the sea or the river or the lake."

Juan touched her sleeve. His fingers came away wet. "You mean like this?" he asked.

"Aye," she answered.

—*The Fish Wife*

May 16

Myla left the group and went up the steps to the long porch in front of the Crow house. This was a good spot to watch the sun come up over the mountains in the morning. She had done so once or twice, wrapped in a blanket and curled up in one of the chairs. It had been a while since she had watched a sunrise. When she first moved here, she had felt so tired and battle-scarred that she had needed the comfort of watching the sun come up and go down every day. She needed to feel the rhythms of this place. Any place perhaps. But this place, this land, was what had rocked her back to sanity.

—*Church of the Old Mermaids*

May 17

Think of something you can sacrifice to this process. To sacrifice means to make sacred. Is there a habit you can "make sacred" by letting it go, giving it up? Your body is your temple, goddess, divinity, world: Are you harming yourself in some way? Can you let it go today? Release it, give it up.

—*The Salmon Mysteries*

May 18

Sara did not look back. Those who were paying attention said later that a whole string of invisibles followed the wagon. Some recognized the good people—the faeries—and others said some of the loa followed. Whoever and whatever they were, they all danced. What a ruckus they made.

—The Fish Wife

May 19

Grand Mother Yemaya Mermaid embraced the New Woman. All the Old Mermaids embraced her, and she embraced them. She felt happy. She felt loved. She felt divine! She hardly had the words to describe how she felt.
—*The Second Book of Old Mermaids Tales*

May 20

"Aren't we all novices in the Church of the Old Mermaids?"

—*Church of the Old Mermaids*

May 21

"Step lightly. Dance hard. Eat your vegetables."
—*Sister DeeDee Lightful Mermaid*

May 22

One by one the Old Mermaids left off whatever they were doing and went into the wash to see what they could see.
—*The Second Book of Old Mermaids Tales*

May 23

Mother Star Stupendous Mermaid said, "We gift you with the ability to release that which does not serve you. And to hold on to the part of your heritage which will heal and nourish you."
 —*The Second Book of Old Mermaids Tales*

May 24

Later that day they had a fiesta at the Old Mermaid Sanctuary. People talked about this party for years afterward. Magic happened. The food served that night cured people of long-standing illnesses. Estranged couples got back together. Children were conceived. Lovers met lovers. Wild animals walked calmly through the patio and house. Desert faeries danced with anyone who would. The music went on all night. The old mermaids came off the walls and joined in the festivities.

—*The Fish Wife*

May 25

"I gift you with the ability to find water and roots wherever you go," Sister Faye Mermaid said.
—*The Second Book of Old Mermaids Tales*

May 26

"I'm speaking truth."
—*Church of the Old Mermaids*

May 27

"The good neighbors helped your great grandmother as far back as forever weave this yarn. It is woven from sunshine and ocean waves, spider webs and mermaid hair, hopes and dreams. It's sprinkled with faery dust, too, it's rumored, so you best be careful what magic you do with it."

—*The Fish Wife*

May 28

"That is part of the recipe of this home-making material. Combine tears and earth. Then stir."

—*An Old Mermaid Sanctuary*

May 29

To Sister Ursula Divine Mermaid, Grand Mother Yemaya Mermaid said, "Into your quilt I sewed all the knowledge of the wild things."

—*The First Book of Old Mermaids Tales*

May 30

"I gift you with wisdom."
 —*The Second Book of Old Mermaids Tales.*

May 31

"Those weren't stories," Sister Rosa said. "They were recipes." She smiled. "Although every good recipe is indeed a story, a story of community, isn't it?"

—*An Old Mermaid Sanctuary*

June 1

"I gift you with enough to eat."
  —*The Second Book of Old Mermaids Tales*

June 2

Sister Faye Mermaid blinked, not understanding what she was seeing. Two tufted ears. This was how the desert faeries looked, according to Annie, The Woman Who Loves Birds. Sister Faye Mermaid heard herself singing. Had she been singing all along? The spot got up and moved out of the light. Something or someone shifted. The desert faery was really a bobcat—or the other way around—and it was looking directly at her as if to say, "You called me. Now what?" The bobcat slowly walked away. It stopped and looked back at Sister Faye Mermaid. She grinned. She couldn't wait to tell the others. *Later.* She'd let sleeping beauties sleep for now. The bobcat desert faery disappeared; Sister Faye Mermaid followed.

—*The First Book of Old Mermaids Tales*

June 3

"Laugh or weep. We swim in your tears."
—*Grand Mother Yemaya Mermaid*

June 4

Usually I take a break to walk the wash. The character in my novel walks the wash, too, so I'm usually walking the wash for her or with her. I'm looking with her eyes as I walk. And she has found some astonishing and ordinary things: bottles, pieces of metal, pieces of plastic, an arrow, a shovel, and more. I've been putting what I find in the novel.

—*Under the Tucson Moon*

June 5

"When they first built the pool, it was the color of the earth because they used earth to create it, but they decided they wanted to paint it. Sister Magdelene Mermaid and Sister Faye Mermaid concocted all kinds of ways to make colors to use to paint the pool. They couldn't use just any paint. You remember that they had already covered most of the walls inside the house with beautiful murals. But they needed to make paint that could withstand the forces of the water. No one is really sure how they did it. Some say the Old Mermaids went out into the desert after dark and negotiated with the desert faeries and other Visibles and Invisibles to use some desert materials. After they combined this and that and got the colors they wanted, they took the paints out under a full moon. They added a secret ingredient to the paint. Then Sister Bridget Mermaid and Sister Faye Mermaid chanted over the paints, and all the Old Mermaids sang a sea chanty or two.

—An Old Mermaid Sanctuary

June 6

Grandmother Sara Mermaid took threads from this piece of quilt and wrapped them around strands of her own hair that she plucked from her head and used for thread. She used these combined threads to make not one, not two, not twelve, but thirteen quilts.
—*The First Book of Old Mermaids Tales*

June 7

Mother Star Stupendous Mermaid said, "I gift you with the ability to be in the here and now. This is powerful magic."

—*The Second Book of Old Mermaids Tales*

June 8

Yes, yes, yes. This was how it was supposed to be. This was her place in the world. For a moment she was balanced between both worlds: She could choose. She could dive into the ocean and feel the freedom within or she could stay on land and live the life she had known for so long. She began to lose her senses. It wasn't a true choice. There was only one way. One wave.

—*The Fish Wife*

June 9

The New Woman realized then it had always been there; she had never lost it. She could never lose her true self.
—*The Second Book of Old Mermaids Tales*

June 10

Another tale goes around that she was once Coyote. Before she ran the nearby hills, most coyotes were loners, but she knew where to get food for the least amount of trouble, and oh, the songs she sang. All the coyotes wanted to be part of her chorus. When she was Coyote, she had known all the magic of the desert and how to trick anyone or anything out of whatever they held precious. One woman said she even tricked her grandmama out of her gold teeth, then gave them back when she couldn't figure out what to do with them. Then she met Señor. He sat on that porch, drinking his juice. And she was smitten. Being that time of month and everything—the full moon—she decided to come and sit for a spell. She had been here ever since.

—*Tales Fabulous and Fairy*

June 11

Sometimes I close my eyes and I can see all these pieces of land like pieces of a quilt. We could link them all up, put them together, and then we would have one beautiful quilt of the world. It's already there, this quilt, so perhaps our job—as caretakers—is to repair the torn pieces, re-stitch those places where the thread has come out, and clear away the debris.

—Under the Tucson Moon

June 12

The Old Mermaids exchanged their finware for skinware and created a house from mud and straw, a house so fine and beautiful that humans and animals of all kinds visited the Old Mermaids Sanctuary to see what they could see.
—*The Second Book of Old Mermaids Tales*

June 13

At dusk, she stood at the edge of the pool and listened to the great-horned owl in the palm tree awaken and try to solve its daily identity crisis, "Who? Who?"
　　　　　　　　　　—*Church of the Old Mermaids*

June 14

"And I swear as the moon rose up over the water, this dark beautiful giant woman with a tail the color of emeralds and rubies rose up out of the water. She reminded me of the auld mermaid I had seen in New Spain. As she came up out of the water, I could feel her power and love radiate to everyone there."

—*The Fish Wife*

June 15

The New Woman hesitated at the entrance to the labyrinth for only a moment before stepping onto the stones. The whole forest seemed to hold its breath as she followed the curving path. And then it began to breathe again as she breathed in and out, in and out. She felt a little dizzy as she gazed down at the stones, yet before long she was near the center of the labyrinth.

—*The Second Book of Old Mermaids Tales*

June 16

"Providing nourishment for other people is a great act of healing, of love. And putting the dishes together so that they taste good and so that they provide nourishment—well, that's magic."

—*The Desert Siren*

June 17

"Into your quilt I sewed a falling star," Grand Mother Yemaya Mermaid whispered to the sleeping Mother Star Stupendous Mermaid, "and the sound of the Old Sea."
—*The First Book of Old Mermaids Tales*

June 18

"And into your quilt I sewed the beauty of moonlight and sunlight wrapped around one another," Grand Mother Yemaya Mermaid whispered to Sister DeeDee Lightful Mermaid.

—*The First Book of Old Mermaids Tales*

June 19

When the Old Sea dried up, the Old Mermaids washed ashore on a desert that was so vast it seemed to travel into tomorrow.

—*The Second Book of Old Mermaids Tales*

June 20

The tide was out, so some of the beach was exposed in spite of the waves and wind. It had grown dark, too, the way it sometimes did when a big storm was coming ashore. The wind was so strong and loud now that Sara couldn't hear her mother, or anything else except the wind. She saw other women on the beach—in a kind of line that she and her sisters and mother were now a part of—walking toward the water. The women's lips moved, and Sara heard something coming from her own mouth. It was a song, a chant, a prayer. It was a plea.

They sang, "We ask those of the Sidhe and those of the sea, calm this storm before it forms, clouds part before it starts, waves calm like a summer's balm, blessings of the sea, blessings from ye, blessings of the Sidhe. Remember us who were once you, sisters, mothers, daughters all, heed our call."

—The Fish Wife

June 21

Satish Kumar was on NPR. It was an interesting interview, primarily because the interviewer just didn't seem to understand Kumar and he sounded frustrated. "What do you mean you're never stressed? What do you mean you never hurry? How is that possible?" And Kumar said he did everything slowly. "Don't you feel the burden of trying to change the world?" Kumar said he wasn't trying to change the world—and yes, indeed that would be a burden. "I serve the world," he said. "I don't try to change it."

Wow. And wow. And more wows! I felt one of those quantum shifts people are always talking about.

To be in service to the world rather than trying to change it. All at once I understood when people said they were in service to God. It didn't have to be a groveling on their knees kind of service. It's what I feel about the Earth, about the world. I do want to be in service to the Earth! Trying to change the world suddenly felt like incredible hubris; me saying I wanted to change the world was like someone else saying they wanted to change God.

—*Under the Tucson Moon*

June 22

Everyone was welcome at the Old Mermaid Sanctuary: the lost, the found, the happy, the sad, the wanderers, the homesteaders, those who sang and those who chirped, those who roared and those who barked, those who burrowed and those who slithered, those who wrote poetry and those who listened to poetry.
—*The Second Book of Old Mermaids Tales*

June 23

Sister Magdelene Mermaid held out an emerald green gown for her. The New Woman stepped into it. Then they led her to a wicker chair with a tall back. The chair was decorated with shells, beads, and flowers. She sat in the chair.

—*The Second Book of Old Mermaids Tales*

June 24

"All the wisdom of the ages can be distilled
into one suggestion: Be."
—*Mother Star Stupendous Mermaid*

June 25

That day, Juan, Sara, and the girls walked into the Old Mermaid Sanctuary as if it was their first time. Sara stood at the wooden gate and ran her fingers over the hand-carved sign hanging there: Welcome to the Old Mermaid Sanctuary. On the side of the gate was an old bell. Juan picked up Nita so that she could ring it. She laughed and slapped her hand against it. Then Emmy did the same thing. Sara opened the gate and walked through it.

Before them was a lush garden surrounded by the curved arches of the three portals. At the center of the garden was a fountain. Two mermaids swam up out of the middle of the fountain. Their tails were entwined and they held hands. Water poured out of their hands.

—*The Fish Wife*

June 26

"You're getting desert eyes, Sister Wild. It's about time."
—*The First Book of Old Mermaids Tales*

June 27

"This was wonderful," I said to Nyalé. "To have a celebration in the middle of a drought is so odd and wonderful."

"What better time!"

"Of course you are right. You can have joy and sadness. That's always been difficult for me to understand. I've always wanted a line to delineate good from bad, happiness from unhappiness. I want things to be simple."

"Perhaps things are more simple than you think," Nyalé said.

I shook my head. "One thing that I've learned is that there are no simple answers to anything."

"Perhaps the simple answer is that all the answers are right."

"Or wrong," I said.

"Have you heard that one butterfly flapping its wings in Australia can cause a monsoon in Japan?"

"Really? Well, finally, the solution to our problems! We need to get a whole bunch of butterflies flapping their wings to cause it to rain here!" I laughed.

"Oya. I said *one* butterfly. Just one."

—*Counting on Wildflowers*

June 28

Someone lifted her and cradled her in his arms. She opened her eyes and saw a tiny patch of gold shimmering through his fur, just like in the fairy tale.

"So you are a man?"

"Shhh," he growled as he reached down and took the pain from her leg.

—*Her Frozen Wild*

June 29

"It's all right," Maggie whispered. "It's all right. This is the place and the time that heals all wounds."

—*The Rift*

June 30

On Friday, a week from when I finished the book, I took the items I had found in the wash, the ones I'd put in the book, and I assembled an Old Mermaid out of them. I called Mario over to help with the tail. We used palm fronds and prickly pear. We both got pricked several times.

When she appeared to be finished, I thanked the spirits and beings of the place, I thanked the Old Mermaids, I thanked everything and everyone, and I offered the art piece as a gift. I then poured out water in the four directions.

—Under the Tucson Moon

July 1

Sara took out the ball of faery yarn and whispered, "The spirits of here and the spirits of there I always honor thee. With this thread, I unweave the spell over me. I untie the ties that bind me to he. Oh, the spirits of here and the spirits of there. With this yarn, I weave a new spell with all my might. I tie the threads up nice and tight. I undo the magic that has been done on me so that I may be forever free."

—The Fish Wife

July 2

The New Woman could feel the power of the land and the dragon and the deep dark water pulsing up through the soles of her feet. She had once felt powerful. What had happened? Had she lost her dragon pearl because she was no longer powerful or was she no longer powerful because she had lost the pearl? Everyone knew that a pearl was the true treasure of every dragon. It was the seat of the New Woman's true power. It was all healing. It was all knowing: the true kind of knowing. Knowing thyself.

—*The Second Book of Old Mermaids Tales*

July 3

Lily took Myla's hand, and they walked through the living room out to the patio. The pool light was the only illumination. Myla opened the door, and the two of them walked to the edge of the pool and looked down at the mermaid. After a few moments, Lily began nodding, as though she were listening to someone speak.

Myla sat near the edge of the pool. Lily sat next to her.

"What are you listening to?" Myla asked.

"The Old Mermaids," she said.

"Oh? What are they saying?" Myla asked.

"Not to be afraid," Lily said. "They sing to me while I sleep."

"What kind of song?"

"A not-be-afraid song," Lily said.

—Church of the Old Mermaids

July 4

At your feet is hard blond dirt, some of it covered in small kitty litter-like rocks. Or maybe you're in a wash, and the earth is like beach sand, only dry. You listen. It is so quiet, the silence throbs. Or is that your own heart? Everything is still, silent, hot. You breathe and hear your own breath. It's just you and Nature. And for an instant, you know you're the same.

—*Under the Tucson Moon*

July 5

And what about that thirteenth quilt that fell into the Big River? Some say it went all the way to the ocean. Some say a whale swallowed it and someone named Jonah used it as a blanket. Some say bits and pieces survived and came ashore here and there. . . . They say if you use a piece of the thirteenth quilt in any other quilt you better be prepared for change. It could turn you into a salmon, a desert faery, or an Old Mermaid.

—*The First Book of Old Mermaids Tales*

July 6

"I love the feel of this earth between my fingers," Sister Magdelene Mermaid said. "It feels so stable and flexible at the same time. And the color! It's sunlight in a brick. Only the Earth could make such color!"
—*The First Book of Old Mermaids Tales*

July 7

In the Old Sea, Sister Faye Mermaid had understood that the sigh of the East Wind meant cold and sometimes enlightenment was on the way. The West Wind most often brought storms and sometimes a sense of calamity. Or an upset stomach. She knew if an eel in the south canyon was wiggling out of its hole happily that either something good to eat was swimming by or it was time to celebrate. If she couldn't see even the tiniest glimmer of an eel's eye because it was so far back into its hole, she knew hard times were coming. (She hadn't seen an eel in an eon before the Old Sea dried up.) She knew by the way the sea fronds brushed up against her if the tide was coming in or out, and she understood all the implications of both. And always, always, she knew the great Old Sea listened to her chants and understood her questions.

—*The First Book of Old Mermaids Tales*

July 8

"I gift you with poetry and music."
—*The Second Book of Old Mermaids Tales*

July 9

"The Old Mermaid Sanctuary is a border place. Like all borders, it is also a threshold. Pilgrims, refugees, artists, storytellers, those who are betwixt and between are welcome."

—*Church of the Old Mermaids*

July 10

"It was just the way they were. It was like breathing to them. They held conversations with the trees and animals and clouds and wind."

—*Church of the Old Mermaids*

July 11

One Raven sister was so old or so young that her feathers and hair were completely white. Her magic came from the Sun and the Stars. One Raven sister was so old or so young that her feathers and hair were the darkest blue-black anyone had ever seen. Her magic came from the Moon and the Earth.

—Tales Fabulous and Fairy

July 12

The cottonwood trees across the street and down a bit stood tall and nearly bare in the moonlight, like tangled members of a Day of the Dead tableau, or a Danse Macabre. Despite this, the air smelled of spring the way only New Mexican air can: like dust, peppers, and the color blue.

—*Butch: A Bent Western*

July 13

I decided to take a walk out into the desert despite the rain. It was nearly sunset, but I went up a trail in Saguaro East. It was so quiet. The sand had become red mud here and there along the trail. Drops of water hung from some of the cholla, completely still, as though they were part of the cactus. I heard and saw several Gila woodpeckers, noisy little creatures way on top of the saguaros. On the ground was a prickly pear pad, partially shriveled, shaped now like a shell; in the "shell" part was a tiny pool of water with sand in it, just like a shell at the beach, a reminder once again that this had all once been an ocean.

—*Under the Tucson Moon*

July 14

"Old Mermaids came in all sizes and all colors. . . . They loved their Old Mermaid bodies, even after that Old Sea dried up and they had to lose their tails and walk on land. Yes, those Old Mermaids loved, Lily my Lily. They loved themselves, they loved each other, they loved the sea and they loved the dried up wash. They loved the cacti and the quail and the coyotes and the mesquite and the Old Man and Old Woman of the Mountains. They loved their neighbors. And guess what else they loved?"

—*Church of the Old Mermaids*

July 15

The New Woman closed her eyes and stepped into the center of the labyrinth. When she opened her eyes, she gasped. She was no longer in the old growth forest. She was in the desert. The labyrinth was gone. She stood on blond desert dirt. A dark woman dressed in a long flowery red and black dress was walking out of the desert toward her.

—*The Second Book of Old Mermaids Tales*

July 16

Her mother reached up to the bonnet on her head and pulled from underneath first one red cap and then another and another; she handed one to each girl.

". . . I wove them with the hair of a sister mermaid, the wool from the Witch McClarny's sheep, and your own precious hair while whispering the fath fith. These will keep you protected and invisible."

—*The Fish Wife*

July 17

"They sang over the bird's wing while they treated it. 'The Old Sea rolls in and washes away the pain. The Old Sea rolls in and washes away infection and inflammation. The Old Sea rolls out and washes away all disease. So say the Old Mermaids. Blessed sea.'"

—*Church of the Old Mermaids*

July 18

"I am most at home where the wild things are."
—*Sister Ursula Divine Mermaid*

July 19

He said she wandered into his view like some sea goddess out of an old story. Of course that description impressed my mother later when he told her.

—The Blue Tail

July 20

"The desert had been dry for a long time. And beyond the desert was dry. People didn't have enough to eat and they couldn't keep their families fed. For some reason, the Old Mermaids always had plenty of food. Maybe it was because they talked to the earth and the sky and the plants and the furred and flying creatures. Maybe it was because of where they were in the bends of the wash. But many came to the Old Mermaids Sanctuary seeking help."

"What did the Old Mermaids do?" Lily asked.

"They opened every door," Myla said. "They opened every window. Sister Sophia Mermaid and Sister Ruby Rosarita Mermaid cooked and baked and served tea and food at the Old Mermaids Tea Shell. Sissy Maggie and Grand Mother Yemaya Mermaid made clothes and blankets and comforters for all who passed by. All of them opened their arms and their hearts and their sanctuary to those in need. When one of the neighbors suggested that they were attracting the wrong kind of people and creatures to the area, Grand Mother Yemaya Mermaid just smiled and said, 'Give us the hungry, the tired, the poor. Give us all those yearning to breathe freely. Blessed sea.'"

—*An Old Mermaid Sanctuary*

July 21

Myla walked the wash looking for trash in the dirt. She looked for treasure too. One man's trash was another woman's treasure. And vice versa, she always said.
—*Church of the Old Mermaids*

July 22

"We could go to an Old Mermaid Sanctuary, baby girl," Grandma Merry said, "and be welcomed and never have to change our ways to be like everyone else, to fit in like a book on a shelf where all the books are the same shape, size, and color and when you open any of them they all tell the same story."

—*The Blue Tail*

July 23

"Because, Lily my Lily, that's the Old Mermaid way."
—*Church of the Old Mermaids*

July 24

It was that kind of place, a ranch but also a way station of sorts—or a sanctuary—where artists, misfits, and other lost souls came to sit for a spell.

—*Butch: A Bent Western*

July 25

Sara did not turn from the stormy sea, even for Ian. The O'Broin women came from the sea and a tempest stirred up all that remained wild inside each of them. Sara was no exception.

—*The Fish Wife*

July 26

As she dropped the comforter over Sister Bea Wilder Mermaid, Grand Mother Yemaya Mermaid said, "Into yours I sewed the magic of the bobcat, the mountain lion, and the lynx."

—*The First Book of Old Mermaids Tales*

July 27

Sister Ruby Rosarita Mermaid decided to make a pot of chili out of the anasazi and pinto beans she had gotten from the Old Man who lived with the Old Woman in the mountains. She talked to the beans all the while she cooked. She always talked to the food. "Beans, beans, we're Mermaid Queens. Make this stew a healing brew."

— *Church of the Old Mermaids*

July 28

It was something to see, this first parade. We all lined up on the beach, dozens of us dressed as mermen, mermaids, and merchildren. I had never seen so much color, so many glittery people. We were all so proud and impressed with one another. Someone began singing a sea chanty, and we walked and danced our way down to the beach.

—The Blue Tail

July 29

"We gift you with your lineage," Grand Mother Yemaya Mermaid said. "You come from a long line of wise women. And they knew how to root themselves to a place. They knew how to walk, dance, move through the world and be full of their own true selves. This is your heritage, too."

—*The Second Book of Old Mermaids Tales*

July 30

"The whole world can be a garden, dawlin'," the Lady With the Galaxy in Her Eye said. "You trying to set down roots? Lessee what I can do."

—*Ruby's Imagine*

July 31

Sister Lyra Musica Mermaid said, "Everyone deserves to be gifted. Everyone should know that they are loved and protected as they go through life. Often people forget their gifts so it's good to be reminded."
—*The Second Book of Old Mermaid's Tales*

August 1

Before they began to eat, Myla looked around the table and said, "I am so glad we are all here together. This is a beautiful place made all the more beautiful by the company. I would like to thank the spirits and beings of this place, especially the Old Mermaids who have made all this possible."

—*Church of the Old Mermaids*

August 2

"Old Woman Who Talked to Cacti had a soft spot for this hard desert, and she welcomed all the creatures who lived on her land or wandered through it. You wouldn't believe what she welcomed and who she talked to. She welcomed mice, rattlesnakes, black widow spiders, scorpions, coyotes, mountain lions. She liked the company. She liked any kind of company. She was able to get used to any kind of being, it seemed."

—*The First Book of Old Mermaids Tales*

August 3

"Welcome," Grand Mother Yemaya Mermaid said, "we have been hoping you'd drop by."
—*The Second Book of Old Mermaids Tales*

August 4

Everyone liked to be invited to the Old Mermaid Sanctuary because it was so beautiful. Many people—even to this day—swear the house was alive. And it was a happy house. Care was taken with every bit of it. The Old Mermaids even asked the land before they built the house where would be the best place.

—*Church of the Old Mermaids*

August 5

"Maybe she was meant to be a tree. A madrone tree, that glorious beautiful maroon color, peaceful and beautiful in these woods alongside the stream."

—*Butch: A Bent Western*

August 6

Myla Alvarez walked the wash that ran through the Old Mermaid Sanctuary, looking for bits and pieces of treasure she could sell at the Church of the Old Mermaids, the table and wares she set up on Fourth Avenue in Tucson every Saturday. It wasn't an ordinary church. It didn't have a building, and Myla didn't subscribe to any dogma. The closest thing to a bible the Church of the Old Mermaids had were the stories Myla told about the Old Mermaids who had washed up into the desert when the Old Sea dried up.

—An Old Mermaid Sanctuary

August 7

"Let the stories begin," Myla said.
—*An Old Mermaid Sanctuary*

August 8

The Trickster, either as Coyote or the bawdy Baubo, is often a character in our own real life stories, whether we like it or not. The way of the Trickster is rarely comfortable. Coyote teaches us that life isn't a puzzle we can solve. It isn't something we can control. Go with the flow, Coyote tells us, and laugh even as you're falling.

—*The Salmon Mysteries*

August 9

"This dirt has everything in it that has lived and will live again," Maire said. "The flowers, the trees, the faeries. My mother gave it to me long ago and said it was a gift for she who would be needing it. She thought it was me, but I never used it. Not once. Maybe you'll know what to do with it."

—The Fish Wife

August 10

Sister Bridget Mermaid said, "I gift you with the ability to ask for help."
—*The Second Book of Old Mermaids Tales*

August 11

I have often said that I'm a stenographer to the imaginal worlds.

Now as I finished this book—my second completed novel in less than a month—I realized I wasn't just a stenographer: I was a mediator between this world and the imaginal worlds. I brought these stories out of there and into here.

—*Under the Tucson Moon*

August 12

"I gift you with the stars, the earth, the moon, and the sun."

—*The Second Book of Old Mermaids Tales*

August 13

"Things change. Get over it."
—*Sister Bea Wilder Mermaid*

August 14

The New Woman stayed with the Old Mermaids for a while longer. She helped where she could. Sometimes she laughed; sometimes she cried. She made art, she made soup, she made silence. She made silence by sitting in stillness and quiet. She liked the way it felt.

—*The Second Book of Old Mermaids Tales*

August 15

It had been a long while since she had realized how beautiful they all were—even though they weren't what they used to be. It had been a long time since she acknowledged how glad she was that she had washed up onto this desert with these Old Mermaids.
—*The First Book of Old Mermaids Tales*

August 16

It seemed appropriate for this pilgrimage to the Old Mermaids Sanctuary, somehow, to have to make it through the fog. To come out the other side.

All my trips to the Old Mermaids Sanctuary are pilgrimages. I go to write. To rest. To be still. To walk with the wild things. To be in the desert is to be present to all things, to the possibility of death. The possibility of life. The fog only reminded me that the veil was thin between here and there.

—Under the Tucson Moon

August 17

"Old Mermaid Sanctuaries are places where beauty, love, and magic still hold sway, where old is beautiful and young is becoming."

—*The Blue Tail*

August 18

"May the beauty of the ocean be upon you, may the coolness of the ocean be upon you, may the joy of a thousand children be upon you, great bounty of the sea be yours, great bounty of our shores be yours, may your lives be hale and fruitful. Welcome, welcome, welcome!"

—*The Blue Tail*

August 19

Sister Ruby Rosarita Mermaid appreciated the New Desert for exactly what it was: dry, sparse, mysterious, dangerous, beautiful. And in the New Desert she discovered her calling, her gift, the thing she loved to do almost more than anything else: Sister Ruby Rosarita Mermaid learned to cook.

—*The First Book of Old Mermaids Tales*

August 20

One night after the Old Mermaids washed ashore in the New Desert, Sister Faye Mermaid could not sleep. She wandered the half-finished house, gliding from room to room, like a ghost, a gentle breeze, or an Old Mermaid swimming in the Old Sea: She was quieter than a cactus mouse. Certainly quieter than the javelinas she smelled and heard snuffling around outside the house. Quieter than the coyotes yipping in the near distance. Maybe not as quiet as the jackrabbit she had seen under the saguaro up the ridge near the Hunter's place earlier in the day. Although maybe he wasn't so much quiet as absolutely still. Sister Faye Mermaid was not still. She was, however, quiet. She did not wish to disturb any of the sleeping Old Mermaids.

—*The First Book of Old Mermaids Tales*

August 21

"That's one of those things that's gotten mixed up in the legends," Myla said. "They tell stories of horrible songs mermaids sing to make men jump in the water. That's silly. Every Old Mermaid—and every person—has her own siren song. It's something she starts creating when she's small. It's a combination of sound and poetry—it expresses her true self. Before the Old Sea dried up, the Old Mermaids would sit on rocks near shore and sing their songs. They are amazing creations, these songs. Completely truthful."

—*Church of the Old Mermaids*

August 22

"I am beginning," the New Woman said, "and I am ending. I am ending old patterns. I am beginning a new life. I need to know how to let go and when to hang on."
—*The Second Book of Old Mermaids Tales*

August 23

I awakes with *the* most full of wonders feels. You knows what I mean? Likes the whole of the Universe is waiting on me, arms open. And can you have an imagine how many arms the Universe would be having? So I gots out of bed and danced around my tiny Place Where I Dream in Mammaloose's house, my bare feet likin' the feel of the wood beneath it, moving just a bit from my weight, bending a little, letting me knows it likes it, too, the wood, I mean, the house, every bit of the world likes my dance.

—*Ruby's Imagine*

August 24

She turned to look at the paloverde who whispered as it moved, "The answers are all here, here."
— *The Rift*

August 25

I would like to see Old Mermaid Sanctuaries everywhere. They already exist in some places. In other places, we need to rearrange things a bit so they can come into existence—or so they can be truly seen, like wiping film off an old window. Old Mermaid Sanctuaries are places where we care for ourselves and each other. Old Mermaid Sanctuaries are places where the sun comes up and the sun goes down. Old Mermaid Sanctuaries are places where the heart opens and love flows in and out. Old Mermaid Sanctuaries are places where cynicism does not exist. Old Mermaid Sanctuaries are places where compassion is a verb. Old Mermaid Sanctuaries are places where you and I live.

—*www.oldmermaids.com*

August 26

Sister Magdelene Mermaid said, "I gift you with love."
          —*The Second Book of Old Mermaids Tales*

August 27

Everyone who lived anywhere near knew that the Woman Who Lived in the House was a force to be reckoned with. She had lived here for as long as anyone could remember and maybe before. All kinds of stories had circulated about her previous life, before she became the Woman Who Lived in the House. Some said she had been La Llorona, wandering the wash in front of the house wailing, until she spotted the Señor on the porch. He looked cool under the verandah, comfortable, drinking his watermelon juice. He asked her to join him, so she did.

—*Tales Fabulous and Fairy*

August 28

"Just trying to figure out how this world works," Sister Bea Wilder Mermaid said.

—*The First Book of Old Mermaids Tales*

August 29

The story goes that as Grand Mother Yemaya Mermaid draped each quilt over a sleeping Old Mermaid, the quilt changed, softening and shifting until it was more than pieces of the New Desert sewn together; each became the yielding healing cloth Grand Mother Yemaya Mermaid had intended it to be. And from that day forward, the Old Mermaids needed only to wrap themselves in their quilts to feel comfort, to feel more like themselves, to recall the Old Sea without sorrow, to feel wrapped up in sunlight and moonlight and the breath of giants and the mystery of the Invisibles—to know the songs of coyotes and the beauty of the desert faeries. It was a great gift Grand Mother Yemaya Mermaid gave to the Old Mermaids.
—*The First Book of Old Mermaids Tales*

August 30

"As long as you swim within the sea of your true selves, you are always Old Mermaids."
   —*The First Book of Old Mermaids Tales*

August 31

Grand Mother Yemaya Mermaid was the wisest of the wisest of the Old Mermaids. She had known the Old Sea was drying up long before anyone else. She knew the paths of the stars in the Old Sky. She knew the difference between the smell of rain and the smell of snow, even before she had ever seen snow. She knew the languages of the birds and the bees and the winds and the trees. And she could sit with the Old Woman and Old Man of the Mountains and discuss the affairs of the mountains, deserts, rivers, and forests with clarity, humor, and insight—as though Old Woman, Old Man, and Grand Mother Yemaya Mermaid had been friends since the beginning of time. And perhaps they had been.

—*The First Book of Old Mermaids Tales*

September 1

If you find any of part of Grand Mother Yemaya Mermaid's thirteenth quilt, sew it into your own quilt and see what happens. And I can tell you how you'll know if the thread or pieces of cloth in your comforter were from any of the Old Mermaid quilts. First, wrap yourself in the quilt. Close your eyes. Can you feel moonlight on your face? Can you understand the songs of coyotes? Do you feel the strength of an eagle coursing through your body? Can you hear the laughter of giants? Do you have an urge to tell stories or sing songs or fall in love with the moon? Does the quilt smell like one of Sister Ruby Rosarita Mermaid's soups, seasoned with possibility and sprinkled with star dust? Do you feel as though you are wrapped in the arms of an Old Mermaid? Take comfort in that. It's the Old Mermaid way.

—*The First Book of Old Mermaids Tales*

September 2

And to Sister Lyra Musica Mermaid, Grand Mother Yemaya Mermaid said, "Into yours, I sewed the music of the stars."

—*The First Book of Old Mermaids Tales*

September 3

And that night, Nita and Emmy slept in their room—the room they had helped paint. Their handprints went all around the bottom of the room. When Renaud had asked them what animals they wanted painted on their walls, they both cried, "Jack the Rabbit!" And so he had painted giant jackrabbits all over the walls, except right above the hand prints. There he had painted Old Mermaids swimming across the walls. Only he said he had painted four, one for each wall, and over night they had multiplied into thirteen.

—*The Fish Wife*

September 4

"I love the colors of ice—the shades of blue and green. I love the sounds the ice makes in the rivers as they begin to melt—as if everything in the universe is collapsing as I watch the sun changing ice into water in slow motion. I like making love in the summer wheat fields where red poppies mingle with the golden stalks, covering field after field with their blush. I like the sound of my own heart as I run through the woods. I like the feel of the Earth beneath the soles of my feet. I think I can be happy for an eternity if only I can touch the woman I love, but I know that isn't true because I will then long for the next touch, and the next."

—*Her Frozen Wild*

September 5

"Hearing a language that isn't your own, that you don't quite understand, is like listening to music. I imagine that's what the sailors used to hear when they passed the mermaids at sea. The mermaids were talking in a different language."

—*Church of the Old Mermaids*

September 6

Mother Star Stupendous Mermaid took the New Woman's hand and said, "I can see by the stars in your eyes that you are not certain why you have come to the Old Mermaids Sanctuary. It is good enough that you are here. Come eat with us and sleep under our roof made of Earth. Tomorrow Sister Ursula Divine Mermaid will take us out into the desert to see what we can see

—*The Second Book of Old Mermaids Tales*

September 7

One of her children, most often a little girl, stumbles upon the cloak one day when she is feeling adventurous and wild, exploring a place in the house her father warned her against. The girl immediately takes the cloak to her mother. "Is this what you have longed for, Mother?" the child asks. "Is this what you have needed?" The woman exclaims in delight. Without a backward glance, she puts on her cloak, transforms into a swan, and flies away home.

—*Swans in Winter*

September 8

I feel more like an Old Mermaid, learning to swim in the ocean of my being, in the old sea that is this world. I am a novice in the Church of the Old Mermaids. I found solace and peace at the Old Mermaids Sanctuary for thirty-eight days. I want to carry that solace and peace with me. The Old Mermaids solve problems differently than I do. I want to learn from them.

—*Under the Tucson Moon*

September 9

Sara had seen her mother's own ball of faery yarn many times since she was a baby. Maire used a little of it in every blanket she made, in every dress she sewed. Tonight the yarn in her box was the color of white sheep's wool, but Sara knew it could take on any color, just like a rainbow.

—The Fish Wife

September 10

"I quite enjoyed the Wisdom of the Desert Faery Tea," Old Neighbor's Husband said. "I feel just a bit wiser myself right now. No desert faeries were harmed in the making of this tea, no doubt."
—*The First Book of Old Mermaids Tales*

September 11

"I gift you with left-handed knowledge," Sister Sophia Mermaid said. "I gift you with the ability to stop thinking and go into the dark."

—*The Second Book of Old Mermaids Tales*

September 12

"All around me, people howled. I laughed and howled again. We had become the Cosmo Clan, or the Red Rock Clan, or the family of the Earth. Whoever we were, we howled together into the night.
—*The Gaia Websters*

September 13

"Beware of this feast, or any truth-telling food. The truth isn't always what we want, moi dear, is it? But you are different, aren't you? You can take it. Eyes wide open. Greet the day. *C'est la vie!*"

—*Coyote Cowgirl*

September 14

They say that Grandma Sara pulled the thread from that thirteenth quilt and made hundreds maybe even thousands more quilts. Everyone who ever got one of those quilts felt great comfort. They say that even today, somewhere, threads from that thirteenth quilt remain—threads that are made up of the strands of hair from a mermaid. And we all know what magic those contain.

—The First Book of Old Mermaids Tales

September 15

The east horizon, above the Rincon Mountains, is a delicate blue, almost turquoise, and I want to wear it, like a dress, with a scarf around my neck the color of the west horizon, splashed with sunset.

—*Under the Tucson Moon*

September 16

"These are places where people like you and me could live, baby girl," Grandma Merry said. "Where we could thrive, where other people like us live—people who are still wild, who are still connected to the great Old Sea and all the wild things."

—The Blue Tail

September 17

"As Grand Mother Yemaya Mermaid listened to the sea in her sleep, the other Old Mermaids saw her tails in the dark—beautiful and luminous, like they had been when the Old Mermaids lived in the Old Sea. They wept and laughed at the splendor of it."

—*Church of the Old Mermaids*

September 18

"Into your quilt, I sewed the nourishment of the Old Sea," Grand Mother Yemaya Mermaid told Sister Ruby Rosarita Mermaid.

—*The First Book of Old Mermaids Tales*

September 19

"A good bean is hard to find. Everything else is easy."
—*Sister Ruby Rosarita Mermaid*

September 20

They traveled in silence as the gray night turned to gold green day. The sky became that perfect blue Butch had never seen any other place except in a New Mexican sky.
— *Butch: A Bent Western*

September 21

Sometimes Grandpa and I would sit in the plaza watching the people go by. He'd nod to this woman or that man and say something like, "I bet she's from the Old Sea. You can tell by the glitter in her hair." Or, "He's definitely from the Old Sea. I hear bells when he walked by. Did you hear them?"

—*The Blue Tail*

September 22

"Do Old Mermaids have to eat oatmeal?"
—*Church of the Old Mermaids*

September 23

It wasn't that the Old Mermaids weren't happy in the Old Mermaid Sanctuary creating their home and making new acquaintances with the furred, the flying, and the friendly. Still, Grand Mother Yemaya Mermaid had seen the tears and heard the longing in the voices of the Old Mermaids when they spoke of their life before the New Desert. Grand Mother Yemaya Mermaid was the oldest of the Old Mermaids, after all, and she wanted to gift the Old Mermaids with something that would bring them comfort all the days and all the nights.

—*The First Book of Old Mermaids Tales*

September 24

"Why does the dirt shine?" Lily asked.

Myla smiled. The Church of the Old Mermaids had no dogma, but Myla did adhere to at least one golden rule: Answer all questions put to her by a five-year-old child with honesty and beauty.

"Well, Lily my Lily," Myla said, "I can't be sure, but I think those shiny bits of sand are star dust—at least that's what Mother Star Stupendous Mermaid told the other Old Mermaids when they first got to the New Desert. They had to sleep in the wash for a while, and Mother Star Stupendous Mermaid told them the sand would keep them warm and give them good dreams because it was made from star dust, shed by the stars the way we shed skin. I'm not sure the Old Mermaids believed her, but they did agree that the star dust was much more comfortable to sleep on than they would have guessed."

—*An Old Mermaid Sanctuary*

September 25

Tulip remembers everything.

She remembers how the dirt in the wash feels on the soles of her feet.

She remembers the sound Old Crow makes when he laughs.

She remembers the kiss of the wind on her cheek.

She remembers to open her mouth when she gets butterflies in her tummy so they can fly out.

She remembers what the trail looks like after desert faeries have been there, so she can track them through the wash as well as the Old Man of the Mountains can track the mountain goats up the east ridge.

And she remembers to breathe, breathe, breathe it all in.

—*The First Book of Old Mermaids Tales*

September 26

Because I'm a writer, I often see the world in metaphor—the land is like our body, the land is a quilt, the land is our mother. But I feel the world in my bones, too. I breathe the world in and out. I take off my shoes and I step on the grass, on the dirt, on the earth, and feel my soles against the soul of the world. I feel the Earth—Nature—beneath my feet like an ocean wave and I know I should grab a surfboard and enjoy the wild ride.

—*Under the Tucson Moon*

September 27

Sister Ruby Rosarita Mermaid believed most problems between people could be solved by sitting around a meal together. The food connected them, became a part of them, and therefore they were connected to one another.
    —*The First Book of Old Mermaids Tales*

September 28

I felt as though joy was bubbling up from the desert ground. I raised the rattle up high and sang. Now was my time. Now was the time for healing. Now was the time for success. My slumber was over; my suffering was over.

—*Under the Tucson Moon*

September 29

Connection with nature is reaffirmed everywhere in an Old Mermaid Sanctuary. Those in need are welcomed. Songs are sung. Enchantments are chanted. Joy is joyful. And dances are danced. That is the Old Mermaid way.

— *www.oldmermaids.com*

September 30

"Do you know what the Old Mermaids say about love? There are always more fish in the sea."
—*Church of the Old Mermaids*

October 1

"Needles for sewing and knitting," her mother said. "One is new and the others are from your grandmother's sewing basket. She got them from her grandmother. They've stayed sharp all these years. The story goes they were made by a smithy who was trying to protect his children from one of the folk who kept stealing the children away. As long as they sewed or kept a needle in their clothes, they were safe from all kinds of thievery, including the faery kind."

—*The Fish Wife*

October 2

"I gift you with the mysteries of the Old Sea."
—*The Second Book of Old Mermaids Tales*

October 3
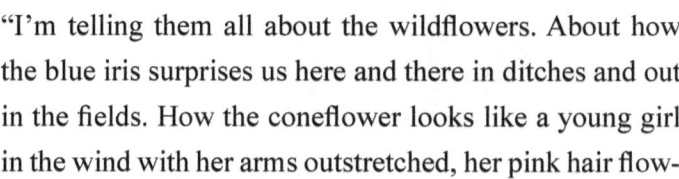

"I'm telling them all about the wildflowers. About how the blue iris surprises us here and there in ditches and out in the fields. How the coneflower looks like a young girl in the wind with her arms outstretched, her pink hair flowing behind her. There's such beauty all around us."

—*Jewelweed Station*

October 4

Grand Mother Yemaya Mermaid laid a quilt over Sister Sheila Na Giggles Mermaid and whispered, "I sewed the strength of an eagle into your quilt."
   —*The First Book of Old Mermaids Tales*

October 5

I had never seen anything as beautiful as my mother and grandmother dancing with me while the cottonwood leaves fell all around us. I heard the fluttering of wings. Then, just before the almost heart-shaped cottonwood leaves touched the ground, they burst into feathers—into golden birds that flew all around us, until the courtyard was filled with us and golden birds breaking free, flying this way and that.

—*Mercy, Unbound*

October 6

The Old Mermaids sang softly near her, their desert comforters wrapped tightly around them. Grand Mother Yemaya Mermaid said, "May you be, may you be, may you be," and she slowly began unwrapping the quilt. I can't be sure of what happened next. I can only tell you what was told to me. But as she unwrapped the thirteenth quilt to drop the bones of the Old Mermaid into the river, the bones slipped away on their own. Only they weren't bones. Some say a salmon twisted out of the quilt and leaped into the water. Some say a faery slid away. Still others say it was the Old Mermaid herself, restored to life.

—*The First Book of Old Mermaids Tales*

October 7

Myla especially liked seeing the mermaid at the bottom of the pool. David Thomas Crow had painted it when his parents drained the pool soon after Myla arrived. The mermaid was beautiful, with black eyes, a peach-colored tail, and tiny multicolored starfish in her wild black hair. She was quite voluptuous and had an uncanny resemblance to Myla, a fact everyone was too polite to mention.

—Church of the Old Mermaids

October 8

And so it began. One by one, neighbors and strangers drifted into the Old Mermaids Tea Shell. Sometimes Sister Sophia Mermaid talked with the visitors for a bit and then recommended a particular tea. Ofttimes she seemed to know just what they needed. Soon the Tea Shell was overcrowded with teatotalers. The Old Mermaids set up tables and chairs outside the Tea Shell.

It was quite a thing to witness, all these people sitting around sipping X Marks the Spot Roadrunner Tea, Sassy Saguaro Tea, Magic of Hummingbird Tea, The Great Horned Owl Hootin' and Hollerin' Tea, West Wind Whimsy Tea, and A Spot of Prickly Pear Tea.

—*The First Book of Old Mermaids Tales*

October 9

"When I was a girl, I believed I was put on this Earth to love. That was it. Then I got older and realized that was kind of foolish."

"A fool is just a person at the beginning of a journey," Mom says.

—*Mercy, Unbound*

October 10

Sister Sheila Na Giggles Mermaid stepped forward first and said, "I gift you with the ability to see the truth." She touched the middle of the New Woman's forehead with her fingers.

—*The Second Book of Old Mermaids Tales*

October 11

One day the ship was rocking and tilting from the backside of a storm; the children were sick and afraid. Sara sat amongst them and said, "Close your eyes, every one of you. You're doing too much seeing with your eyes. You've forgotten the ways of the fey folk and you've only been gone such a short while. Don't you remember running in the woods and hearing the trees creaking and moaning as they danced with the wind? Ahhh. Ya hear that sound again, don't you? Aye."

—*The Fish Wife*

October 12

Today I had one of those silent desert days. I walked the wash and walked the wash, just like Myla, looking for trash I could turn into treasure. I figured out what I was going to write next and listened to my feet crunching over the sand. Quail walked daintily, all in a row, up and out of the wash. Doves fluttered from the trees as I went by, startling me and them. Then I sat outside near the Quail House. I listened to the whoosh-whoosh-whoosh as a crow flew overhead. I heard the owl call out twice. Thrashers and other birds made themselves known. Desert cottontails hopped here and there and everywhere. Once in a while I heard the horses snort or whinny. Clouds moved overhead, putting me in and out of shade. Nothing could have been grander.

—*Under the Tucson Moon*

October 13

"I thought that was only a fairy tale," Sara said.

"And don't the fairies know a sight more than we do," Maire said.

—*The Fish Wife*

October 14

Ruby McGonagle leaned over, unbuttoned her left shoe, and slipped it off. She unrolled her stocking. She glanced at the door and then she took off the stocking. Sara looked at her toes. They were slightly webbed.

"Selkie," Sara whispered.

—*The Fish Wife*

October 15

After a while, Grand Mother Yemaya Mermaid stopped singing and began weaving love and healing and nourishment and comfort into the quilts she was creating. "May you never know hunger," she said. "May you know great joy. May you be filled up with love. May you dance and laugh. May you know the touch of moonlight on your brow. May you know the love of a good man. May you know the love of a good woman. May you know the love of children. May you know the love of the stars, and the moon, and the sun. May you know the peace of a blue sky. May you have the curiosity of a crow. May you have the happiness of an Old Sea or New Desert full of Old Mermaids."

—*The First Book of Old Mermaids Tales*

October 16

A coyote crossed the road in front of them, about fifty feet away. The coyote stopped when she got to the other side and looked at them for a second. Butch stared right back at her. The coyote looked like she had something to say.

Apparently she thought better of it, because she trotted off into the scrub.

A road runner followed a few seconds later. The bird stopped and looked at Butch. *"Know the way."*

—*Butch: A Bent Western*

October 17

And so it was that the New Woman came to the Old Mermaids Sanctuary one day. She was standing on one side of the wash one moment; then in the next, she walked across the wash and into the sanctuary. She immediately felt at home. She knew this was the place she needed to be. This was what she had been looking for all her life. And now she was here.

—*The Second Book of Old Mermaids Tales*

October 18

Just about then, she saw the sign, "Welcome to the Old Mermaids Sanctuary."
  —*The Second Book of Old Mermaids Tales*

October 19

"Fear has no sisters, but I have many."
—*Sister Lyra Musica Mermaid*

October 20

One of the Old Mermaids put a cowrie shell necklace over the New Woman's head and around her neck. The Old Mermaids lined up in front of her: It was an Old Mermaid line, of course, which meant it snaked around the pool. "Remember, Sister Mermaid," Grand Mother Yemaya Mermaid said, "that many of these gifts you have had all your life. Now they will become clearer to you."

—*The Second Book of Old Mermaids Tales*

October 21

Everyone knew the Raven sisters. They came from a long line of wise women and men. When the Raven sisters went into the desert—by wing or by foot—they did not want any kind of company. What they did in the desert was a mystery; it was part of the cycle of the place. The Raven sisters helped keep the world in balance.

—*Tales Fabulous and Fairy*

October 22

Grandma Crow had told her that road runners could lead you to safety if you were lost, even though their X-marks-the-spot prints were somewhat confusing. If you weren't lost, best not to follow them.

—Butch: A Bent Western

October 23

"I'm like this because you always encouraged me to follow my dreams," he said. "You told me money wasn't everything. You said I should find beauty in the world and follow it to the ends of the Earth if need be. And to me, there is beauty all around in this place, at the end of the Earth."

—*The Desert Siren*

October 24

Some bird Butch couldn't see and whose song she didn't recognize called out from the madrone. Butch smiled. Everything was so bright and clear. The small white flowers on this madrone looked like bells, and she was pretty certain she could hear them ringing.

—*Butch: A Bent Western*

October 25

"Don't be nervous," Louie told Sister Ruby Rosarita Mermaid. "Don't give it a thought that the cohesiveness of our entire world depends upon this night and your soup."
 —*The First Book of Old Mermaids Tales*

October 26

My mother told me that when she was a girl, her mother used to whisper stories about the ocean to her late at night. Mom would wake up to find her mother leaning over her, spilling stories into her ear, stories about mermaids and Old Mermaid Sanctuaries that were hidden in plain sight all over the world.

—*The Blue Tail*

October 27

"I gift you with the knowledge that you are an Old Mermaid and that you always have a place and a home with us. I gift you with the mysteries of the Old Sea."
—*The Second Book of Old Mermaids Tales*

October 28

"You believe in mermaids?"
—*Church of the Old Mermaids*

October 29

Eventually I will get to hear the desert silence. It is different from any other silence. How to explain it? It's a desolate and comforting silence. And when you hear the sound of another creature, it's as if you're all in it together—you're all in this place surviving and thriving and figuring it out. We're all *compañeros*.

—*Under the Tucson Moon*

October 30

But something happened that day as this bottle—at least I think it was this bottle—fell into the pool and its contents mixed with the water in the pool. The Old Mermaids felt a moisture in their beings that they had not felt since they left the Old Sea. And in the water all around them was suddenly the flashing of mermaid tails. I can't be sure, but the story goes that all the tails of the Old Mermaids were visible again, and they were creatures of the water for a time. It wasn't that they went back to what they had been. Instead, they recognized that they were still themselves, whether they were in the water or in the desert.

—*The First Book of Old Mermaids Tales*

October 31

I had to remember that the wild was always in me. I didn't have a parcel of land to care for. I had me. I had my words. Maybe in some way, that was a help to the world. I hoped Carlos could keep his land wild, for his sake but also for the sake of the world. We will always need wild places and wild keepers.

—*Under the Tucson Moon*

November 1

"Have you gone looking for the thread?" Luisa asked. "The magical thread from the thirteenth quilt?"

—*An Old Mermaid Sanctuary*

November 2

Once upon a dusty time, a young woman walked down a long dirt driveway toward the Earth-colored house with a long wide front porch. Beside the house was a paloverde tree, all green to gather in and process the sun, and a mesquite tree, whose roots reached clear down to springs that gurgled up and became rivers in China, or so some supposed; on the other side of the house, a saguaro stood, two arms up as if a bandit were asking for all its cash and bonds. Behind the house in a tall palm tree, an owl asked the young woman, "Who, who?"

—*Tales Fabulous and Fairy*

November 3

"I love your crow's feet."
—*Church of the Old Mermaids*

November 4

"I gift you with the ability to be nourished," Sister Ruby Rosarita Mermaid said.
>—*The Second Book of Old Mermaids Tales*

November 5

"I gift you with the ability to find delight every day," Sister DeeDee Lightful Mermaid said. She opened her hands and yellow flower petals spilled onto the New Woman's lap. The New Woman laughed and clapped her hands.
—*The Second Book of Old Mermaids Tales*

November 6

The New Woman still wore the clothing of the sea, only now the scales had changed into luminescent threads of purple, green, indigo. A string of white beads and tiny colorful seashells wound its way through her dark hair.
—*The Second Book of Old Mermaids Tales*

November 7

When the Old Sea disappeared, many of the kin of the Old Mermaids washed up on shores far from those they loved. Some of the scattered remembered the Old Sea and the Old Ways; some of them remembered nothing; and some of them remembered bits and pieces of the life they had lived.

—*The Second Book of Old Mermaids Tales*

November 8

"The next morning, Grand Mother Yemaya Mermaid said she had had a wonderful sleep and glorious dreams of the Old Sea. Sister Lyra Musica Mermaid and Sister Sheila Na Giggles Mermaid hung the sea shell from the ceiling, right over the bed, so that Grand Mother Yemaya Mermaid could hear the Old Sea every night from then on."
—*Church of the Old Mermaids*

November 9

As we drove, I stared at these beautiful mountains and felt such awe and love for them. On the radio, Paul Carrack was singing "The Living Years," and tears started flowing down my face. I wanted more than anything just to fall to my knees on the sweet hard earth and curl into a ball. Thinking about touching the earth made me feel better. What I want to do with my life is to be able to stand my ground no matter what happens. I want to be able to face life, look at it and know what it is, and not pretend it is something else.

—*Under the Tucson Moon*

November 10

"*Abracadabra.* I think I have the glad feels today. I think that I see miles and miles of swamp filled with alley gators and egrets and fishes and worms and bugs and Rooted People and Flying People and human people, and the ground is squishy and mushy and it can soak up a lot of water. And this city is part of it all. The air is so clean, we just want to keep breathing so we can drink it in along with everything else . . . 'cause all the people here loves, loves, loves everyone else and knows we has to keep the air and water and earth clean. . . . And there's no more poor people. Not because they goes to live somewheres else. No! Everyone has jobs they likes and cares about. They have work that inspires and heals them. They have homes of beauty. And the Home of the Big Oaks and the Flying Horses is even better than before, with green spaces all over the city so that the city itself is a green space. I can see it. I can see the parties and the food and the laughter and the love. I loves, loves, loves it. Can you see it? Can you feel it? Can you make it happen? Yes, yes, yes. This will be the Place Where We Renewed the World."

—*Ruby's Imagine*

November 11

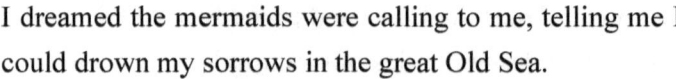

I dreamed the mermaids were calling to me, telling me I could drown my sorrows in the great Old Sea.

—*The Blue Tail*

November 12

"I'm not going away, Lily my Lily," Myla said. "And even if I did, even when I'm gone, the Old Mermaids are with you. They're in your heart. And mostly, they're in the stories."

—*An Old Mermaid Sanctuary*

November 13

"Sing, dance, create.
If you have to choose one, do all three at once."
—*Sister Bridget Mermaid*

November 14

Sara ran her hand over the smooth gray lid and the blood red hinges. Were the hinges made from wood, too? Her fingers touched the mother-of-pearl clasp shaped like a mermaid; the "s" of the mermaid's tail fit over a tiny piece of shell to hold the lid to the bottom of the box. Sara carefully moved the mermaid and opened the lid.

—*The Fish Wife*

November 15

The Old Mermaids whispered to the plants as they walked. They sang softly to the birds, to the sky, to the ground they walked on. It seemed as though they flowed across the rough ground, like water flowing over an empty riverbed. The New Woman could see that the Old Mermaids from the Old Sea had found a connection to this New Desert. She could see they felt genuine love for the land and her creatures.

—The Second Book of Old Mermaids Tales

November 16

I smiled. I could not plant all the trees, or empower all the women, or change the way people worshiped. I could not stop the wars. But maybe I could remember how to dance.

—Tales Fabulous and Fairy

November 17

"The Old Mermaids had tile in the kitchen and bathroom and in funny places in the walls all over the house, so you might look here and see a flower blooming from the tile or you might look there and see a cardinal flying. They painted scenes from the Old Sea on the walls. And scenes from the mountains. Valleys. The desert. These paintings on the walls were so realistic, Lily, that you would swear you could walk right into them and keep on going."
—*Church of the Old Mermaids*

November 18

"In this bowl is the most healing food," Sister Ruby Rosarita Mermaid said. "I always talk to the plants before I harvest them. I always sing to the spirits of the food and ask permission to use them, ask them to imbue the food with nourishment and healing. And I created this soup just for you."

—*The Second Book of Old Mermaids Tales*

November 19

"Of all the seas in all the worlds, we're so glad you swam into our Old Sea."

—*Church of the Old Mermaids*

November 20

I have always believed this place would heal me. I have always believed the Old Mermaids would heal me. They have in so many ways. This is where I belong, at least for now; for this moment in time, I am under the Tucson moon once again.

—*Under the Tucson Moon*

November 21

"I had that dream again the other night," Myla said. "Where I'm in the Old Mermaid Chapel and the desert is singing to me."

—*An Old Mermaid Sanctuary*

November 22

"Well, Lily my Lily, I suppose each treasure hunt is different for each person," Myla said. "I ask the wash and the Old Mermaids to show me what is here for me on this day. Often I find things as I walk. At this time of year when it's been dry for a long time, the pickings are slim. So sometimes I just stop. I don't know where or when. I stop when it moves me, and I close my eyes and breathe. When I open my eyes and look around, I almost always see something I hadn't seen before."

—*Church of the Old Mermaids*

November 23

Mario opened the window and we heard one of the border guards saying, "I heard the more accurate translation of Crazy Horse's name is Enchanted Horse. Now doesn't that sound better than Crazy Horse?"

—*Under the Tucson Moon*

November 24

On this day, you should take time out to pray. You don't have to pray to a deity, certainly, especially if you don't believe in one! I think of prayer as a song I sing to myself and the Universe. I chant (pray) as a way to center myself, to ground myself in the here and now. This is another way of deepening as you follow the path of the Mysteries.

—*The Salmon Mysteries*

November 25

The wash is not really empty. It's filled with sand. Fairy sand, maybe. It got all over my shoes. My soles. Filled up my soul with fairy dust. Old Mermaid dust.
—*Under the Tucson Moon*

November 26

The sky was overcast now, suddenly, and Sara wondered if it was magic that made it so. She whispered the fath fith, the ancient charm to make her invisible and keep her from harm. Her mother had taught the fath fith to them when they were young. Sara used it to walk amongst the deer in the forest and swim in the cove with the seals. She also whispered it when she walked down to the cove, mostly so none of the village boys could see her and follow.

—*The Fish Wife*

November 27

Sister Sophia Mermaid and the others went out into the desert collecting for the Old Mermaids Tea Shell. They went when the moon was brightest, or just before the sun came up, or mid-afternoon—you know, those betwixt and between times, the sleepy times when all manners of creatures wander through your world, this world, other worlds. And they would whisper to the Visibles and Invisibles and ask if they could have a bit of coyote song or desert faery magic or rabbit runnin' or cloud essence for their teas. They set out clear glass jars until they got an answer. Then they emptied the jars into cloth bags Sissy Maggie Mermaid, Sister Lyra Musica Mermaid, Sister Bridget Mermaid, and Sister Faye Mermaid had decorated and sang to and laughed over. Sister Sophia Mermaid carefully labeled each bag, then dropped them into the appropriate jars when she returned to the Old Mermaids Tea Shell.

—*The First Book of Old Mermaids Tales*

November 28

Sara began dreaming again. This time she was swimming in the auld sea as it dried up and she walked up into the new desert, near the Old Mermaid Sanctuary. Her children were running around the patio. The house was full of people. They laughed and sang and worked and played. And the cacti, paloverde, and mesquite moved and danced slowly to music only they could hear. Two desert faeries sat in the sand drinking tea. They looked up at Sara and invited her for a "spot a tea." Her girls called to her and she went running into their arms.

—*The Fish Wife*

November 29

"This is called a dreamcatcher, Lily my Lily," Myla said. "If you put it in your room, it'll take away all the bad dreams. A Native American healer gave one like it to the Old Mermaids when they first came to the sanctuary. It was all new to them, and some of them were afraid. Sister Laughs A Lot Mermaid, who was the youngest, had bad dreams. When the medicine man gave her this dreamcatcher, the bad dreams went away."

—Church of the Old Mermaids

November 30

"Mermaids are sea goddesses who got some bad press," Mom told me. "Your father saw me for who I truly was. Sea goddess. Mermaid. Po-tay-toe. Po-tah-toe."
—*The Blue Tail*

December 1

Grand Mother Yemaya Mermaid understood that "things" would not make the Old Mermaids happy. Still, she knew that each place had a way of being, a natural flow, a kind of enchantment about it. And the Old Mermaids needed help finding the flow of this seemingly still and prickly New Desert, they needed help discovering the enchantments of the New Desert, and just maybe a found object from their new world would help with this.
—*The First Book of Old Mermaids Tales*

December 2

"I'm not swimming in tears or anywhere else if I don't get some food."

—Church of the Old Mermaids

December 3

Then a breeze whispered to her, bringing the smell of bear. She looked up. Amongst the trees, a thick tall yellow-brown figure walked. The slender white trees almost looked like the bars of a cage, only this being was not contained. Asya blinked. It was a woman striding through the forest, wrapped in fur, walking on the ice-snow without slipping.

A woman who was not caged or contained.

Asya glanced in the direction from where she had come and then over her shoulder at the hill which hid her village from view. Then she looked through the trees again. The woman watched her.

Asya released the birch from her embrace and followed the woman deeper still into the wild.

—*Her Frozen Wild*

December 4

"I see dreams as gifts," Myla said. "Like moving art pieces. Literally moving, I mean. You don't always know what a painting means, but you can still enjoy it or dislike it."
—*Church of the Old Mermaids*

December 5

Right this second the sun has plunged into the Pacific Ocean hundreds of miles away and the splash is painting our desert sky first lavender and now rose. And the desert is so quiet I could hear a feather drop. Now the sun is adding gold to the structures near and far. The tree trunks which hold up the roof of the Quail House are black tinged with gold. In this light, they looked edible. Dark chocolate.

Everything shimmers.

—*Under the Tucson Moon*

December 6

"I heard it in the Wind and the Wind never lies."
—*Butch: A Bent Western*

December 7

Sara liked the desert immediately. It was familiar in a way she did not quite understand. The silence throbbed in her ears like a distant ocean. In the forests and on the plains they had crossed, Sara had heard and sometimes seen coyotes, but the ones in this desert were different from those. These ones were leaner, more curious. They stopped and watched Sara and the others, seemed to be contemplating whether they wanted to stay and chat for a while.

—The Fish Wife

December 8

"I wasn't singing, sweetheart," Sister Faye Mermaid whispered. "I was just breathing."

"Same thing," Sister Laughs A Lot Mermaid said.
—*The First Book of Old Mermaids Tales*

December 9

Sister Sophia Mermaid would write on the special board something like: "Two cups of Dances With Joy Tea for the price of none." Ah, you should have been there that day. People danced inside and all around the Tea Shell. Most people agreed that Laugh Yourself Silly Tea Day was the most fun, although Love the One You're Always With Tea Day was a close second.

—*The First Book of Old Mermaids Tales*

December 10

It is a very old world. And the sea is the oldest of all. Who knows what is true about such things and what is false?
—*Church of the Old Mermaids*

December 11

"I told you the Old Mermaids were still here."
—*Church of the Old Mermaids*

December 12

I went outside and stood in the street. It was so quiet. Full of peace, it seemed. No one around I could see. Just me and the rain and the sense of strange that comes before every storm—you know what I mean? Like something is gonna happen. May not be something big. May not be something small. But things are changing.

—*Ruby's Imagine*

December 13

"We have all felt homeless at one time or another," Sister Sophia Mermaid said. "As Grand Mother Yemaya Mermaid said, we could all use some sanctuary now and again."

—*The First Book of Old Mermaids Tales*

December 14

What if we each pledged to care for a plot of land? It could be a square foot, the footprint of the place where we live, a piece of property we own, or a park we love. We would care for these pieces, these plots, these Earthly parcels, like we would care for our fingers or our arms or our legs: We would recognize that it is all a part of us, and as the land is cared for, so are we.

—*Under the Tucson Moon*

December 15

"Grand Mother Yemaya Mermaid is the wisest of wise," Myla said. "She is one of the ones who is a moon beauty, like your great grandmother. And her skin is as dark as night. Darker. She is so grand that she had two tails before the Old Sea dried up."

—*Church of the Old Mermaids*

December 16

I found the edge of the blanket and began unwrapping. First the tail was exposed—a fish tail, wooden, with rose-colored scales. The body curved up, and small yellow wooden hands cradled a wooden basket next to bare pale gold breasts. I unwrapped a head and I saw the whole mermaid. She had medium-length brown hair, red lips, marble eyes—brown and realistic looking. On her forehead and around her head was a gold and red crown. She had a smile like Mona Lisa's: small and mysterious.

—*The Blue Tail*

December 17

She called it the Church of the Old Mermaids because her mother told her when she was a child that the desert had once been a vast sea. She liked imagining that the mermaids had not dried up when the sea did; they merely changed their attitudes. And maybe their skin and finware.

—Church of the Old Mermaids

December 18

It is true: in the desert you can't hide anything. It's all out in the open. One way or another, if you stay long enough, the desert will show you the truth. Every year here I learn things about myself and the world I didn't know before. Sometimes they are things I would rather not know.

—Under the Tucson Moon

December 19

Sister Magdelene Mermaid said, "She just needs some lovin'. That is in great supply here at the Old Mermaids Sanctuary."
—*The Second Book of Old Mermaids Tales*

December 20

"Are you another lost explorer?" the Woman Who Loves Birds asked.
>—*The First Book of Old Mermaids Tales*

December 21

"First we honor the spirits and beings of this land. We honor the east and the element of air and pray for illumination. We honor the south and the element of fire and ask for the will to go forward. We honor the west and the element of water and ask for the ability to love and dive wholeheartedly into our deepest feelings. We honor the north and the element of earth which surrounds us this day and ask for peace and the ability to be still and silent."

—The Gaia Websters

December 22

She felt the Old Sycamore behind her supporting her. She felt the Earth beneath her. She felt the twinkle of the stars above her. She felt the presence of the Old and New Wild Things all around. She felt completely at home with herself, and she felt herself completely at home. She felt, she felt, she felt.

—*The First Book of Old Mermaids Tales*

December 23

To Sister Magdelene Mermaid, she said, "Into your quilt, I sewed the love of the mountains, desert, and sky."
—*The First Book of Old Mermaids Tales*

December 24

"You are part of Nature."
—*The Second Book of Old Mermaids Tales*

December 25

It was a tiny church. As round as can be, built mostly from stone. As far as Sara could tell, everyone from the sanctuary and everyone else they knew came and helped. Every one of them went into the chapel and painted something: mermaids, seashells, fish, trees, lions, bears, coyotes, little girls with fish tails and wings on their hearts.

—The Fish Wife

December 26

"I remember now how I was part of the Old Sea, how I lived in beauty with my mermaid sisters, how every cell of my body was filled with joy and love and pure ecstasy. How we swam in our deepest darkest most beautiful places."

—*The Blue Tail*

December 27

"They painted the pool with special colors. They made it look like their old home in the Old Sea. It was dark and watery and blue and green and filled with Old Mermaids and sparkling treasures. Not the kind of treasures you always hear about, not gold and silver. Old Mermaids didn't care about those kinds of things. No, it was filled with colorful sea stars, jellyfishes, all kinds of glittery fish, dolphins, whales, and rock formations that looked like castles. It was beautiful! People said that every time you looked at it, it was different. One minute it seemed like it was mostly green, the next blue or indigo. It was a marvel. And it lasted for as long as the Old Mermaids were here, maybe even longer."

—*An Old Mermaid Sanctuary*

December 28

"Aunt Delilah said we came from a long line of sea horse sirens—like horse wranglers. . . . It was our heritage to protect and preserve these amazing creatures, she told me. She said being a 'sea horse siren' was like being a horse wrangler only it required a belief in the existence of magic—and the ability to sing your own siren song. She'd tell me this stuff and I'd listen with one ear. With the other ear, I was thinking 'there goes crazy Aunt Delilah.'"

—*The Desert Siren*

December 29

Butch started to walk away from the buildings and into the night, forgetting why she was there, only wanting to get closer to the sound of the coyotes and the mother ditch. Suddenly the north sky lightened, and Butch looked up. A shooting star streaked across the sky. Butch laughed. If Crazy Betty saw that falling star she'd be full of space alien stories for days.

—*Butch: A Bent Western*

December 30

"Could anyone be an Old Mermaid?"
—*Church of the Old Mermaids*

December 31

"Ah, look at those stars," Sister Star Stupendous Mermaid said. "That bunch looks like a dragon tonight." The stars did wind through the night sky the way a dragon might. "I often feel as though a dragon is nearby, a part of this earth. Different from the dragons we had in the Old Sea. This dragon is at home in this desert and never longs for the Old Sea. She is content with her life as it is now. That's always a process, isn't it?"

—*The Second Book of Old Mermaids Tales*

All quotes were harvested sustainably from the following books (and one website) written by Kim Antieau, with help from the Old Mermaids:

The Blue Tail

Butch: A Bent Western

Church of the Old Mermaids

Counting on Wildflowers

Coyote Cowgirl

The First Book of Old Mermaids Tales

The Fish Wife

The Gaia Websters

Jewelweed Station

The Jigsaw Woman

Her Frozen Wild

Mercy, Unbound

An Old Mermaid Sanctuary

www.oldmermaids.com

The Rift

The Salmon Mysteries: A guidebook to a Reimagining of the Eleusinian Mysteries

The Second Book of Old Mermaids Tales

Tales Fabulous and Fairy

Under the Tucson Moon

About the Author

Kim Antieau has written many novels, short stories, poems, and essays. Her work has appeared in numerous publications, both in print and online, including *The Magazine of Fantasy and Science Fiction, Asimov's SF, The Clinton Street Quarterly, The Journal of Mythic Arts, EarthFirst!, Alternet, Sage Woman,* and *Alfred Hitchcock's Mystery Magazine.* She was the founder, editor, and publisher of *Daughters of Nyx: A Magazine of Goddess Stories, Mythmaking, and Fairy Tales.* Her work has twice been short-listed for the Tiptree Award, and has appeared in many Best of the Year anthologies. Critics have admired her "literary fearlessness" and her vivid language and imagination. Her first novel *The Jigsaw Woman* is a modern classic of feminist literature. She has also written *The Gaia Websters, Butch, Her Frozen Wild, The Fish Wife,* and *Church of the Old Mermaids.* Kim lives in the Pacific Northwest with her husband, writer Mario Milosevic. Learn more about Kim and her writing at www.kimantieau.com.

About the Cover Artist

Nancy Norman resides in the Pacific Northwest. She has received many state, local, and international art awards. "My favorite work has the intense irrational reality of a dream," she says. Nancy has exhibited her work at Dragonfire Gallery in Cannon Beach for the past ten years.

The Thirteen Suggestions

Get the starfish outta your eyes, sister.
Sister Sheila Na Giggles Mermaid

Step lightly. Dance hard. Eat your vegetables.
Sister DeeDee Lightful Mermaid

Things change. Get over it.
Sister Bea Wilder Mermaid

Fear has no sisters, but I have many.
Sister Lyra Musica Mermaid

She who laughs a lot laughs a lot.
Sister Laughs A Lot Mermaid

I am most at home where the wild things are.
Sister Ursula Divine Mermaid

Sing, dance, create. If you have
to choose one, do all three at once.
Sister Bridget Mermaid

A good bean is hard to find. Everything else is easy.
Sister Ruby Rosarita Mermaid

Go with the flow—and watch out for waterfalls.
Sister Sophia Mermaid

You ask me to tell you about love? Showing is so much better.
Sister Magdelene Mermaid

Laugh or weep. We swim in your tears.
Grand Mother Yemaya Mermaid

All the wisdom of the ages
can be distilled into one suggestion: Be.
Mother Star Stupendous Mermaid

The rest is . . . mystery.
Sister Faye Mermaid

www.ingramcontent.com/pod-product-compliance
Lightning Source LLC
Chambersburg PA
CBHW030049100526
44591CB00008B/74